The Mind and

The Mind and I

Reflections of a Psychoanalyst

JAMES JOYCE

McFarland & Company, Inc., Publishers

Jefferson, North Carolina

ISBN 978-0-7864-9762-1 (softcover : acid free paper) ∞
ISBN 978-1-4766-1936-1 (ebook)

LIBRARY OF CONGRESS CATALOGUING DATA ARE AVAILABLE

BRITISH LIBRARY CATALOGUING DATA ARE AVAILABLE

On the cover: *inset* the author; other images © iStock,
Ingram Publishing, Photo Objects/Thinkstock

Printed in the United States of America

McFarland & Company, Inc., Publishers
Box 611, Jefferson, North Carolina 28640
www.mcfarlandpub.com

To Jean, Veryl, Dick and Caye—
mentors, colleagues, friends

"Psychoanalysis is a crutch. At this time in my life that's just what I need is a crutch."—Woody Allen, moviemaker

"Life is short. Psychoanalysis is forever."—Jean Rosenbaum, M.D., author

Table of Contents

Table of Contents

Preface

This afternoon I saw my last patient for the final time so it is the appropriate day to begin this book. This is a symbolic beginning, no more than a few hundred words, because soon (it's almost 6 o'clock) I am going to celebrate the end of my psychoanalytic practice.

I'll be eating and drinking like a hedonist tonight—steak, lobster, baked potato and Caesar salad. I'll be washing it down with Johnny Walker Black, instead of wine, because I hate wine. After dinner I'll sit in front of the fireplace with a snifter of Grand Marnier and conjure up images of my patients' faces, with their smiles and their tears, and remember our times together.

Since I practiced in three distinct areas of the United States—the West, Midwest and South—I was fortunate to have a diverse group of patients. I treated rodeo riders, businessmen, real estate women, policemen, politicians, doctors, lawyers, artists, college professors, a drug dealer, a cowgirl, nurses, Navajos and a hooker—to name some. The identity of the patients presented will be disguised, of course, anonymity being sacred in psychoanalysis, but the psychodynamics they reveal are true.

Some of my patients were rich, some were poor—I always had one *gratis* case. Some were old, some were young—occasionally I saw children. A few were especially interesting; a few were mind-numbingly boring, but most were between those extremes—the average Joes and Janes of everyday life. But whether sophisticated city-slickers or down-home country folk, they all shared at least one thing in common: they had trouble in their minds.

I will be using the pronoun "he" when referring to analysts because

1

it is easier to write that way, not getting bogged down with the cumbersome "he or she." But today as many women as men practice psychoanalysis and, in my experience, women are usually better at it. They are more intuitive.

There is a vast difference in both depth and scope between psychoanalysis and psychotherapy, but I lump them together because each uses talking, instead of drugs, as the primary vehicle to alleviate mental illness. Drugs are the bailiwick of psychiatrists, who are medical doctors. Few psychiatrists that I have known have the time, training or inclination to listen to their patients talk beyond hearing their symptomatic complaints. Dispensing medications, and monitoring the effects, is the customary psychiatric approach to mental health problems. Medications can be miraculous for symptom abatement and thank God we have them, but they don't address underlying causes—unless those causes are biological and not environmental (most are environmental). Psychiatrists and psychotherapists are often wary of one another, yet both have much value, especially when they work together with patients—the psychiatrists to even them out; the therapists to sort them out—over time.

People are of three minds: (1) Conscious—what we are thinking about at the moment; (2) Preconscious—that which we can easily bring to the conscious mind; and (3) Unconscious—what we have forgotten. The unconscious should not be confused with the "subconscious." That term was popularized by Hollywood in the early 1900s and essentially has no meaning. If your mental health therapist uses the word "subconscious," I suggest you flee.

And what is the unconscious? It is our emotional engine, made by nature, then individually customized and fueled by our experiences. As it drives us through life it is the major determinator for sadness or joy, frustration or peace, success or failure as a person. The unconscious mind is as much a part of us as the blood that courses through our veins … yet we can feel neither.

Because our unconscious minds are formed when we are infants, toddlers and little kids (until about age six), few of the details are accurately remembered. So we make them up. If our re-creations are too far removed from truth, our pasts become personal myths. Therein lies the seat of so many emotional problems. The discrepancies between the realities of our childhood experiences and our current perceptions of them can drive us crazy. We'll spend lots of time on the unconscious. It is the most powerful force in human nature, yet it is cloaked in subtlety, mystery, misinformation and paradox.

I often refer to myself and fellow psychoanalysts as "shrinks." Although some colleagues take offense at this term, thinking it unprofessional, I think it's appropriate because we shrink problems or, more accurately, we shrink the neuroses in which they dwell. I did not know the original derivation of this slang word so I called the National Association for the Advancement of Psychoanalysis, our psychoanalytic group in New York City. I asked the executive director where the work "shrink" came from. She didn't know, nor did others she queried, but all guessed it had something to do with disgusting practice of shrinking dead people's heads. I like my take on it better.

I wrote this book for readers to understand what it's like to see a shrink. They'll learn it is not a scary thing to do. On the contrary, it is always interesting, frequently fascinating and often lots of fun. They will also learn what it's like to *be* a shrink. Most of us psychoanalysts are not gifted people. It is only our training that sets us apart. Our job is to hold up mirrors to our patients' words. We listen as the patients talk and we don't cast judgment. Emotional re-adjustments can only come from the patients. It is their job to judge themselves.

Emotions are confusing, untrustworthy and frightening to many—a milieu of feelings that sometimes cannot be coped with and may, indeed, overwhelm. This book explains where emotions come from and how they affect us. (Our emotions, by the way, are not uniquely ours. We are mostly carriers for our forebears.) The book was also written for beginning analysts and therapists and those in training, with the hope they may learn from my experiences—especially my mistakes.

Psychoanalysis is properly referred to as a science, but it is not a science of the Newtonian tradition. Psychoanalysis is more akin to the relatively new and more encompassing science of quantum physics. Both arrived on the scene at the same time, the first decade of the twentieth century. They revolutionized their respective disciplines. Quantum physics introduced quarks—sub-atomic particles that don't always behave as expected, driving scientists nuts. Psychoanalysis introduced the unconscious mind—the wellspring of our emotions, which can drive everybody nuts.

Let's get a drink.

1

Colorado

Splitting to the Rockies

We like to think we are in charge of our lives, and sometimes we are, but there are times when events occur beyond our control that take us places we didn't know existed and from which there is no turning back. That's how I became a psychoanalyst. It was unplanned (undreamed of), and sometimes I wish it had never happened. Psychoanalysis is a dangerous profession.

The year was 1973 and moving to Colorado seemed like the reasonable thing for my wife and me to do to save our floundering marriage. Colorado had become a destination for disenchanted young couples who were no longer satisfied with their careers, lifestyles and, especially, each other. I quit my lucrative job as a real estate salesman at a posh golf resort near Clearwater, Florida. We put the house on the market, sold all the furniture and the Cadillac, and traded the Lincoln Continental for a used Volkswagen mini bus. (We got money back.) We loaded up the boys, ages two and three, and headed west, 1,942 miles, to the small town of Durango. We'd heard that Colorado could save marriages. We decided to give it a try.

The Colorado marriage-saving theory was quite popular in those days and thousands of people bought into it. Influenced by John Denver's hit song "Rocky Mountain High," we headed to the mountains leaving behind family, friends and all trappings of our previous lives. We would start afresh in the pure, crisp air of the Rockies unencumbered by our pasts and the baggage that went with them. My wife and I had come to realize that we'd been seduced by materialism and the acquisition of "things." Things that played to our pride, were devoid of joy, and had gotten in the way of "us." That life was now over. We would build a little cabin in a high valley and somehow eke out a living. We wouldn't need much, the simple life was what we craved. We were in complete agreement about this and it was, in fact, the only thing we agreed on. Colorado would save our marriage.

I do not remember the trip to Colorado except for the crossing of Wolf Creek Pass, elevation 10,856 feet. On flat land the Volkswagen was a slow-moving vehicle, going uphill it went even slower, but going up a mountain the pace was excruciating. Fortunately, prior to ascending the pass, a Colorado native told us, "Whatever you do, don't stop. If you do you're finished. You'll never be able to get forward motion again." This advice was invaluable and somehow we made it, reaching the summit going 3 mph, the Volkswagen screaming like a wounded fox. The vehicle would never be the same.

On top of the pass was a pullover area where we stopped to collect our nerves and allow the cars behind us to proceed normally. There must have been a hundred of them, the drivers and passengers glaring at us as they passed. Some gave us the finger.

In Durango we rented a nice furnished apartment and began the search for our building site. We contacted a realtor and told her we wanted something remote, inexpensive and pretty. She gave us a knowing look and in no time at all she found it—two and one-half acres of land with a river on one side and a 500 acre cattle ranch on the other. it was in a high valley ten miles north of Durango and here's the best part: It already had a log cabin on it! The rustic, rundown little building had been built before the turn of the century and oozed with charm. We agreed it was perfect and bought it on the spot.

Before moving in we decided to expand it just a bit and hired a contractor. He was very creative guy with lots of swell ideas. Plans were discussed and pored over and construction began. Six months later our little rustic log cabin was now mostly inside of the house we built around it and on top of it. Our new home was beautiful, dramatic and had some very creative touches. It also cost a fortune. Meanwhile, the house in Florida remained unsold.

We traded the beat-up Volkswagen for a new four-wheel-drive

Chevy truck. The four-wheel-drive would be necessary when the snow came. This vehicle also made economic sense. With a truck I could now buy feed in bulk for the twelve hogs, two steers and goat I had begun to raise, quite a savings over buying feed in sacks. New furniture was purchased for all the rooms in the house and Jenn-Air appliances for the kitchen. By now we had learned Durango was not the cow town we had envisioned. It had lots of classy, sophisticated people, our kind of people, so to be sure we wouldn't be mistaken for hippies, we also bought a Buick.

It was early spring when we got settled into our new home. The valley and surrounding mountains were tranquil and beautiful. Golden and bald eagles frequently glided overhead. Deer and elk were in abundance. The creek sang to us as did the wind through the aspen. If there is such a thing as a therapeutic setting we had found it. Colorado was working its magic and we were doing great.

Originally I'd planned to start small as a farmer, buying just two pigs at the auction, but a neighboring farmer heard I liked pigs, so he offered to sell me ten of his young ones for a very good price. What I didn't know (and never in a million years would have thought of) was because six of the ten little pigs were males they would have to be "cut" to have any value. When I learned this gruesome fact I hired a professional cutter.

"You roll him on his back then sit on him and hold him his legs apart," he said. I had not intended to be part of the cutting procedure, but he said it was necessary so I did what I was told. The man then started slicing the little pig's testicles off and you have never heard such screaming in your life! It was horrific and heart stopping and my testicles were only inches from the little pig's teeth.

We eventually got all six of them cut and I vowed never to do that again. For many weeks afterwards I kept hearing a "snip" sound, like a scissors in my mind. I thought I was going insane. I learned later I was experiencing castration anxiety.

As fall arrived and the aspen leaves turned we knew we'd settled in heaven. Huge swatches of the mountainsides were covered with brilliant gold, interspersed with the deepest green of fir and spruce. Everywhere we looked we were awestruck by the beauty. If God made a quilt ... well ... he had.

When winter set in we thought we were in good shape because our new home had not one but three wood burning fireplaces. We quickly learned that all three needed to be going all the time, to heat the incredible amount of air space we had created. (The living room ceiling was twenty-three feet high.) This was an all but impossible task and the wood, not cheap, had to be purchased. After a while, exhausted from hauling logs, we relied on the electric baseboard heaters to keep us from freezing. In January, as the temperature went below zero, the electric bill hit $750. You know that silver disc in the electric meter with the black mark on it? You should have seen it spinning around and around inside the glass cover. Neeyow, neeyow, neeyow! Watching it made me sick.

Finally we got an offer on the house in Florida for $4,000 less than what we paid for it, but no problem. Getting out from under that monthly payment would take a lot of pressure off our dwindling cash. But when the buyers returned for one last look before closing they discovered that the long-vacant house was now crawling with cockroaches. They quickly backed out of the deal. I flew to Florida to get the house professionally de-bugged. While there I also dropped the asking price, and after a year on the market the house finally sold for $12,000 less than we paid for it. We were going financially backwards at the speed of the electric meter and our marriage again turned sour.

We Need More Help

It was now necessary to get a job. I found one selling condominiums, making about one-fourth what I made in Florida, and working six days a week from 8 a.m. until 6 p.m. *Sayonara* to the simple life. Things were not going as planned and divorce was discussed on a regular basis. It was one of the few topics we could discuss in a rational, civilized manner; it was making a lot of sense to both of us.

About this time we learned of an organization in Durango called the Institute for Child Development and Family Guidance. Marriage counseling was one of the services offered and we signed on. We were given individual appointments; my wife's on Monday, mine on Tuesday.

1. Colorado

We were told we would be seeing the same psychoanalyst, a woman, but we would not see her together. "It's hard to be completely open and candid in front of your spouse when there are problems," was the explanation given. This, we agreed, was reasonable.

I had had and encounter with a shrink once before. It was a brief interview with a U.S. Army psychiatrist, which was necessary to qualify for the Army's flight program. But that wasn't the same as seeing someone about personal problems. The Army psychiatrist (I figured out years later) was simply trying to determine if I was crazy enough to fly an airplane in combat. I passed his test. This encounter, however, would be very different. The sessions would last an hour, and there would be at least five of them. This concerned me. What could I possibly talk about for five hours? I was certain that 90 percent of our marriage problems were my wife's. Even pointing out all of her faults shouldn't take more than an hour and then there'd be four more hours of dead air. I became apprehensive.

When I came home from work on Monday night I noticed that my wife was in a great mood. I asked her if she'd seen the analyst and she said, "Did I ever!" I asked her what it was like and she said, all smiles, "We're not supposed to talk about it. You'll find out tomorrow."

"Can't you even give me a hint?"

"No."

I did not like the way this was shaping up. I quickly went over my wife's faults, and my own, and was ready to concede that perhaps it was only 80 percent her fault that the marriage was a flop.

That night we had friends to our home for dinner. I made the announcement that this would be the last night of my life that I could say, "I have never seen a shrink." I said this to get a laugh, but I was really trying to cope with my nervousness. The concept of "seeing a shrink" was, to me, the most foreign of concepts. If a guy's got problems he tells them to a friend. If they're serious he talks to a priest. If he's really screwed up he calls his mother.

The next day I told my boss I needed time off to see a professional about my marriage. He was sympathetic and encouraging. He told me I could have all the time I needed for this worthy endeavor then added that every marriage in the state of Colorado was on the rocks, his own

9

included. He, too, had seen a shrink about his marriage problems but it didn't do any good.

Armed with this mixed message, I reported to the institute for my appointment. At exactly 11 o'clock the door of the waiting room opened and an attractive woman came out and introduced herself as Veryl Rosenbaum. She shook my hand firmly and asked me to please follow her. We walked down a hallway past some closed office doors and I couldn't help noticing that my psychoanalyst had a very pretty rear end. I was ashamed of myself and hoped she couldn't read my mind. What if she asked if I was leering at her? As a Catholic I knew that lying to a priest in Confession would nullify it. I assumed the same would be true of psychoanalysis. You can tell, by now, I was really out of it. Why on earth would she ask if I noticed her butt? It embarrasses me to admit these thoughts and, of course, she didn't ask.

In the room were two chairs facing each other and a black leather couch against a wall. She told me to have a seat and I leapt into one of the chairs. No way was I going near the couch.

Veryl began by asking me questions: my age, where I grew up, did I have brothers and sisters, were my parents still alive, how did I get along with my family—simple stuff. I began to relax. When I said something that I thought was humorous she thought so, too. She had an easy way about her and we chatted freely. She'd grown up in a blue collar neighborhood in Detroit. I told her I'd grown up in the same kind of neighborhood in Chicago. A camaraderie was building between us and before I knew it the hour was over and we hadn't even mentioned the marriage.

I enjoyed my first session with a psychoanalyst and was looking forward to the next one. I felt I could say practically anything to this attentive, non-judgmental listener and she wouldn't interrupt as a friend, a priest or my mother would surely do.

My wife and I were told (warned) up front that marriage counseling by a psychoanalyst was not necessarily designed to save the marriage. It was stated that some marriages should not be saved, as they were poisonous to the participants, including the children. The analysis was conducted to examine the marriage objectively so the couple could decide if it should continue. This came as disturbing, shocking news to us and we contemplated ending the therapy before it was too late. But too late for what? The marriage was already a wreck. We continued on.

Psychoanalysis is about individual emotional growth and when married people begin to grow there is no guarantee they'll grow closer together. It's possible they'll grow farther apart and that seems to be what happened to my wife and me. As months of analysis went by, our differences were magnified and we both agreed it was time to throw in the towel. So the marriage ended—the ending enhanced, paradoxically, by the isolation of Colorado and the bright light of psychoanalysis. The two things we'd hoped would save it.

When I began practicing I saw numerous patients who'd fled to the mountains hoping a different and beautiful setting would solve their problems. They came from New York, California, the Midwest, Texas and everywhere else attempting to leave their problems behind. It never worked. Whether those problems were with spouses, or carried solely within, they re-emerged after a year or so of living in the beauty. We can't escape our minds anymore that we can escape our hearts.

And guess who else go divorced after moving to Colorado? Our prime mover, Mr. Rocky Mountains himself, John Denver.

I hope we got points for trying.

2

Why I Became
a Psychoanalyst

It Made Sense

I had become a dedicated analysand (patient) and continued to see Veryl after my wife and sons moved back to Florida. I became hooked on the process, intrigued by the simple truths it revealed, and hungered for more. I also began to harbor a fantasy of one day becoming a psychoanalyst, and I confided this to Veryl. A few months later the psychiatrist-psychoanalyst and author Jean Rosenbaum, M.D., Veryl's husband and founder of the institute, invited me to join the next class of candidates to begin formal training to become certified psychoanalysts. He offered to be my mentor—the highest of compliments. I was euphoric.

But the euphoria was short lived when it occurred to me that I might first have to become a psychiatrist to become a psychoanalyst, which meant medical school. There was no way I'd be able to go back to college to get my GPA up, especially taking pre-med courses. I thanked Jean for the offer but told him I simply wasn't smart enough to become a doctor.

He laughed and said I did not have to be a medical doctor to be a psychoanalyst and, in fact, I shouldn't be. "Doctors are too desensitized by med school. They usually don't make good analysts. It took me years to get over med school. Those cadavers...," he sighed.

"I don't understand," I replied.

"Medical doctors," Jean continued, "are electricians, mechanics, plumbers, engineers and chemists for the body. They are not trained to treat the mind. Analysts deal in fears, memories, and guilts. Those schooled in liberal arts are more attuned to those venues. Doctors are trained to deal with tangibles. We work with feelings."

I wasn't sure what he was talking about but it sounded good. Then he outlined what I would have to do to complete training and be certified. The guidelines were established by the American Board for Accreditation in Psychoanalysis and had to be fulfilled in an ABAP accredited institute, such as the one he founded.

There would be a minimum of 300 hours of personal psychoanalysis and another 300 hours of on-the-job training with patients under supervision. I would be the analyst, alone in the room with a patient, and would then meet with my supervisor and brief him on what took place. He'd critique my performance and offer guidance for the next session. Thirty-six credit hours on theory and technique were required, as was a master's degree from an accredited college in one of the liberal arts. "Plan on five years," he said. "No problem," I replied. I was determined.

At that time Goddard College had a branch in Denver and I enrolled. Although some class work was involved, the essence of the program was writing a thesis under an accepted mentor's guidance.

I plunged into the program with Jean as my guide. My thesis, entitled "Man: The Creator," explained how the analytic process unleashes latent creative drives. I also added tons of information on psychoanalytic theory, so the thesis would be long enough to be approved. Our Goddard faculty advisor, a man named Fred, told us he would not be reading our theses, he'd simply be weighing them. "Make 'em thick," he said. I couldn't tell if he was serious or not, so I loaded mine up with words, words and more words.

During the 1970s mental health therapies of every description were rampant. One weekend in Pagosa Springs, Colorado, we twelve Goddard classmates met with Fred for a weekend of lectures and discussion. We also took turns reading parts of our theses to get feedback from our peers and Fred. Most of us were pursuing a master's degree in one of the mental health disciplines—mine was in modern Freudian psychoanalysis. We were an eclectic group: traditional Freudians, humanists,

Jungians, Adlerians, behaviorists, primal screamers, you name it, and there was lots of not-so-good-natured give and take. Each of us felt our discipline had the key to fixing all that ails the human psyche. In turn we believed the other disciplines were seriously flawed.

Toward the end of the last session when I'd finished reading from my thesis one of the students, a surly young woman, was sitting in her muumuu glaring at me, all the while stroking her girlfriend's leg. When she could no longer contain herself, she said, "Sigmund Freud was a pervert and you shouldn't be wasting your time, and ours, by writing about that asshole."

Her remarks hurt my feelings and I went for the throat, unkindly commenting about her lifestyle, and that did it. The room went up for grabs. The students started yelling, swearing and even crying. Those pent up hostilities were now off the leash, with even the heretofor quiet ones now spewing venom. There was much finger pointing and glaring, mostly at me. I was called old fashioned, out of touch with the new reality and too conservative to be a therapist. Someone suggested I apologize. I suggested he cram it.

When we quieted down I turned to Fred and asked him to comment on our "discussion." I felt I had an ally in Fred. He was black, straight, an athlete and an all around cool dude. He looked around the room and said, "You all make me sick. You are a bunch of fucked up people who plan to go out and help another bunch of fucked up people." At the time I resented Fred for saying that. Now it makes me smile.

I finished my thesis, which weighed in at just over one pound, and received my master's. I continued my personal psychoanalysis, completed the required hours of training and went into private practice.

God Didn't Do It to Me

Having mentioned that I had become intrigued by the simple truths of psychoanalysis, I should explain what was so intriguing. Here's an analogy: A quarterback makes a "T" with his hands to signal "time out." The game isn't going well, his team is being badly beaten. Changes must be made or it will probably get worse. He needs time to re-group, rethink and to confer with his coach to find out what is going wrong with the original game plan.

Psychoanalysis provides people a time out from the ongoing process of life. It is like a time warp, a safe haven, creating an environment for reflection and honest (sometimes excruciatingly so) talk. Where they've been, who they've become and how they got there are candidly discussed. What forces moved them this way and that way as they rushed through life? Who were the people who influenced the decisions they made?

I'd never thought of life that way. I simply thought of myself as a guy who did the best he could in whatever situation he found himself and fate, or God, took care of the rest. I went to grammar school, then high school, then college, then the Army, then the war, then into marriage, into parenthood, and then got divorced. Not once did I stop to look back. Too busy. Now I was looking back and, yes, I was intrigued.

I had never stopped to consider that God's plan for me probably did not include living two thousand miles away from my sons. How the hell did that happen and what part did I play in it? Who, other than God, made me me? Psychoanalysis had answers to these questions that made sense. I learned I was the end result of many *people* and *events* going back to my birth. It wasn't "God's will" that I would wind up a divorced man in Durango, Colorado. Rather it was a series of decisions that I made, spawned by unconscious forces of which I was now becoming aware. This newfound knowledge was at once exciting and scary. Exciting, because I could take control of the rest of my life. Scary, because the burden of responsibility was placed squarely on my shoulders. I would no longer have anyone else to blame—including my ex-wife.

When I was five years old, a ten-year-old girl in our neighborhood told me, and other little kids, that there was no such thing as Santa Claus. "The adults make him up," she said to the horror of my playmates. But I was not horrified. I liked this idea of no Santa Claus, but I couldn't tell if she was lying so I decided to ask my dad. I knew he would level with me when asked a direct question. And true to form he admitted Santa Claus was not a real person and that the presents under the Christmas tree really came from Mom and him. I can't tell you how relieved I was, because I knew my mom and dad would not withhold gifts no matter how bad I was. I had been terribly concerned about Santa Claus because he really didn't know me and I was totally at his mercy.

I had the same feeling of relief shortly after encountering the psychoanalytic process. To me, God and Santa Claus had a lot in common. We mortals were at their whims as they rewarded good and punished evil. I quickly learned it wasn't a fickle God who put me in my current fix, but rather a series of decisions that *I* made which were greatly influenced by my relationship with my parents, their relationship with each other, and their relationship with *their* parents. And there were other identifiable people from my past who contributed to my current predicament. Causes and effects were clearly pointed out. I began to see that my unconscious mind was an accumulation of personal psychic events that compounded over the years and now mightily influenced my current thoughts, words and deeds with remarkable, embarrassing consistency. Psychoanalysis made sense.

I also learned, to my dismay, that the unconscious mind is not concerned with what's best for me; it has no conscience in that regard. It is only concerned with keeping itself intact. It resists change of any kind—good or bad. Like a phonograph record it spins the same emotional tunes day after day and year after year. It is oblivious to its host's feelings of sadness or joy, frustration or peace—except to make sure nothing changes. It, like gravity, is pervasive and constant. In terms of people, it is the most powerful force on earth. Globally it causes wars; around town it's the catalyst for crime; within the family it's responsible for pettiness, jealousy, selfishness and rage.

During my training I experienced how the unconscious can be changed, however, when the messages it plays are destructive. The "program," so to speak, can be re-written when the instances that caused the destructive behavior are intellectually remembered, emotionally re-felt and put into perspective. But this takes an enormous amount of honesty, trust and time. It also entails looking at loved ones presently, and from the past, in an objective, often unflattering light. This is terribly difficult to do.

I Surrender

I will never forget the session with Jean when those concepts struck home—literally. I loved my mom, dad, brother, sister, grandparents and did not want to say anything negative about them. And I certainly didn't feel anything negative about them. They were on their proper pedestals in my mind, with their goodnesses intact and their flaws minuscule. I was unwilling to view them in any other light. It didn't seem right. It was also frightening because to do so would alter the core of "me." Of course I knew from my studies that those pedestals must be removed for growth to occur, but that knowledge was intellectual and didn't really apply to me. I was different. My family was wonderful, unlike the families of Jean's other patients. Thus I reached an impasse in my analysis.

Then something snapped and for the first time I was aware of my emotional defenses. I actually *felt* them and Jean pointed out that if they didn't come down I was wasting my money and his time. I had been clinging to the belief that I was basically a loving man, living a good life, one who had the best of upbringings and was, overall, a happy, well-adjusted guy, even though the evidence showed otherwise.

I don't know where I got the nerve, but I said to him, "Okay, you prick, I will let you break me down and take me apart. I just hope you have the wherewithall to put me back together."

Jean smiled and said, "Jim, you are not Humpty Dumpty. I can't break you and I don't have the power to take you apart. All I can do is help you find the truth about yourself. That's what psychoanalysis is all about. Truth."

I surrendered.

As I began practicing I realized that my impasse with Jean was typical. Almost all of my patients came up on that moment when earnest heartfelt conversation ended and was replaced by defensiveness as the unconscious began to show itself. "What do you mean my mother's love was lacking? What do you mean my father was distant? What do you mean I resented my sisters and brothers?" Or if taken to the present, "What do you mean I withhold my love from my children and am dishonest with my spouse?" These defensive statements are from the unconscious, which is saying, "Whoa!" It recognizes truths surfacing and truths cause growth and growth means change and *the unconscious does not want to change.* This is everyone's battle and I committed to join in my own fray. It was intriguing. It made sense. But, boy, was it hard to do.

3

Can a Catholic Do It?

Yes

Early on psychoanalysis was dubbed "The Jewish Science" because nearly all of the first practitioners were Jews. Although Christianity was fathered by Judaism there are some striking differences between them. Jews don't concern themselves with an afterlife; Christians are preoccupied by the concept. Slap a Jew in the face and be prepared to be slapped back. Slap a Christian and he will turn the other cheek. (Not really, but we're supposed to.) A Jew believes "getting even" is appropriate when he has been harmed by his fellow man. Christians believe in forgive and forget. (Not really, but we're supposed to.)

Christians believe they sin by having impure thoughts about the girl in short-shorts walking down the street. Most Jews believe that's nonsense. Christians believe that Jesus, a Jew, was the son of God, born of a virgin, who purposefully got himself crucified in order to redeem mankind for the sins of Adam and Eve. Jews don't think so and are still waiting for their messiah. When it comes to the Bible, Christians put their emphasis on the New Testament, relegating the Old Testament to being old news. Jews consider the New Testament to be an interesting read, at best. There are numerous other differences between the two religions.

During my analysis my Christian-Catholic religious beliefs were rarely mentioned and if they did emerge Veryl shrugged her shoulders, implying they essentially had no analytic value. "Psychoanalysis does not concern itself with religious beliefs," she once said. "They are out of its realm." Indeed, the issues we worked on in my personality that were self-diminishing and psychic energy draining seemed to have nothing to do with my religion. A Methodist, an atheist or a Hindu could have the same negative unconscious impulses that I had: needing to be the center of attention; needing dozens of friends; needing to be correct on all topics; needing to be in control of those around me; needing to be liked; needing to be needed; needing to be the best in those areas in which I chose to compete. I could go on, but you get the picture. I was needy, and that had nothing to do with my religion.

While religion was not a factor in my personal analysis, I would soon begin practicing the Jewish science and I was somewhat concerned about it. I had been raised in the strictest of Catholic families in the strictest of Catholic environments. My roots are embedded in an Irish neighborhood on the south side of Chicago from 1940s and '50s. No place on earth has ever been, or ever will be, more Catholic, and my family took it even farther. There were holy water fonts at the entrances to the rooms in our home. My older brother, a seminarian, drew life-size pictures of the Crucifixion, the Agony in the Garden and the Ascension of the Blessed Virgin into Heaven on the walls of our bedroom. My father wouldn't miss Sunday mass, or daily mass during Lent, no matter what. My sister taught, voluntarily, in one of the worst inner-city public schools. She was a saint. And my mother, a daily mass and communicant, became the president of the Chicago Archdiocesan Council of Catholic Women. I was raised pure Catholic.

When I was invited to go into training I took this concern to my mentor, Jean, a non-practicing Jew. Like Veryl, he also shrugged it off, but was a bit more talkative.

He explained that psychoanalysis and the Christian religion are not, at their essence, opposed to one another and they actually can be quite complementary. Both have the desire to bring peace to the mind and soul, and both are acutely aware of the healing powers of truth and forgiveness. He said that there are probably more Christians than Jews practicing psychoanalysis today, so it's no longer the Jewish Science. When dealing with my patients' religious issues his advice was to realize the religious material was probably being used as a defense against some other, deeper, emotional problem. "Just listen for clues to unconscious forces and don't, of course, impose your beliefs on your patients. That would be a sin." He chuckled.

He mentioned "forgiveness" which is, or is supposed to be, a hallmark of the Christian faith. "Father, forgive them for they know not what they do" were some of the final works Jesus spoke. "Forgive us our trespasses as we forgive those who trespass against us" is in the prayer he taught us. All Christians know the importance of forgiveness, but many would be surprised to realize that forgiveness is also a hallmark of psychoanalysis. Without it the job is not complete.

When "Joe" begins psychotherapy his analyst will be acutely interested in his "history." He'll ask him to start at the beginning of his life and walk him, step by step, up to the present. He'll want to hear Joe's earliest memories, his relationship with his parents, and their relationship with each other. Siblings, aunts, uncles, grandparents, teachers, clergy, coaches, and people in Joe's childhood neighborhood will be of keen interest to his analyst, and in the telling of his story Joe can begin to determine who was good to him (and for him) and who was not, and in what instances. Some people who should have been really good to Joe when he was young may not have been, and if Joe was unaware of this before therapy he will certainly learn it as his therapy progresses. This process makes patients angry at those people and brings that anger to the surface, from the unconscious to the conscious mind. They'll get pissed (sometimes really pissed) at those who did them wrong and it won't matter if those people are presently alive or dead. This is a goal of psychotherapy; patients finally being able to angrily express in words those hurtful feelings buried years ago.

Let's say a patient's father was one of the culprits in her less than perfect childhood. He was a weekend drinker and on more than one occasion had been heavy-handed with her and verbally abusive. But long ago she forgot about his abusiveness and today he's a kind and gentle old codger. If memories of his meanness emerge she quickly dismisses them, saying something like, "Forgive and forget." But her unconscious mind has never forgotten her shame and mortification (and the anger) when dad was slapping her around and telling her how worthless she was. When she and her therapist take the lid off these powerful memories and feelings she will, hopefully, again feel enraged at the way her drunken father treated her years ago.

And it is good for her emotional growth to stay angry at him for weeks, months, maybe even years depending on the depth of the pain. But someday (there is no hurry here) she must resolve her feelings and accept them as a reality of her life. She'll do this by verbalizing them, re-feeling them and putting them into an adult perspective in her conscious mind. Then she can really forgive her father for being what he was, a flawed human being who was made that way by those flawed human beings who raised him (her grandparents), who were made that way by those flawed human beings who raised them (her great-grandparents) going all the way back to the aforementioned Adam and Eve.

I had a psychoanalyst colleague who had a terrible childhood history. Knowing the highlights of his past, I found it amazing that the man became a productive adult. Physical abuse, sexual abuse, and verbal abuse took place regularly in his early years, not ending until he joined the military at age fifteen. His parents helped him lie about his age, which was probably the only nice thing they ever did for him. Years later, shortly after his father died, my colleague used his influence to put his mother in a nursing home hundreds of miles away from where he lived. He told me that he hated his mother and for twenty years he had no contact with her. When he died he didn't know if his mother was still living. People who knew his mother said she was the worst of the worst, a woman who was cloying, sexually obsessed, bitter, and a pathological liar. She was also a drunk. My colleague could not get past his rage at his mother. He died, by the way, estranged from his own children.

Forgive: But Don't Rush It

I know what you're thinking. How could this psychoanalyst, who had to go through psychoanalysis himself, not get to closure with his feelings toward his mother and forgive her? You have a good point. My colleague believed to the end that his situation as a kid was so horrible that he was unique and did not have to eventually forgive his mother.

He was wrong, of course, and his personal analysis was incomplete. He was also a flawed analyst. We therapists cannot take our patients to places we haven't been. Because he never got to his "forgiveness stage" his patients didn't either, and their analysis was also incomplete.

What does this have to do with being a Catholic and a practicing psychoanalyst? When I began practicing I would be faced with a fundamental conflict between my church's teachings and what I learned as a candidate. For instance, the church considered divorce, birth control, sex outside of marriage, adultery, masturbation, and abortion serious sins, but these were simply opportunities for analytic material in my profession. It took me a while to get it into my thick skull that I was not a priest, a judge, or a parent. I was a psychoanalyst and this is the kind of stuff we worked with: "You're cheating on your wife? How come? Don't you love her? You're jacking off four times a day? What's making you so anxious? You've had five abortions? Why do you keep getting pregnant; have you got something against babies?" Good analytic material will show itself as the patients' unconscious minds emerge, and their moral judgments would remain their responsibility, not mine.

The forgiveness part took me longer to grapple with, however. We Catholics believe that Jesus was nailed to a cross and hung from it in pain beyond imagination, at the same time asking his father to forgive his torturers because they "know not what they do." Meanwhile, back on the couch, I would encourage my patients to re-experience and express aloud their anger at their drunken father because he whacked them around and belittled them. In other words, I would encourage my patients to be un–Christ-like.

But my patients and I would eventually get to the forgiving part, and the healing would begin. Although it took Jesus only seconds to forgive, it might take patients months and years to do so. I could live with that.

It also became clear to me that the church that preached instant forgiveness was woefully unaware of the depths and intricacies of the unconscious mind. To encourage people to blithely forgive those who were supposed to be loving and nurturing to them but were, in fact, treating them horribly sets people up for mental illness. They are harboring emotional lies.

Forgiveness is a great healer—coupled with truth it's the ultimate healer—but only if it is done with insight, a solid understanding of ourselves and our tormentors, and over a long period of time. Forgiveness can be a crippler to the emotional system if it takes place rapidly and, "Because you're supposed to, it's the Christian thing to do." In this instance it isn't done, anyway. The "forgiver" is simply using words and religious beliefs that are devoid of feeling. These words and beliefs tighten the lid on anger and bury it in the unconscious, sometimes making an emotional time bomb and always contributing to a feeling of "there's something wrong with me."

Religious Matters

Shrinks have been accused of attempting to replace religion with psychotherapy and some have, especially beginners who are particularly zealous. As enthusiastic as I was, and remain, about the miracle of psychotherapeutic treatment, I never believed it was a replacement for religion. They are separate entities: one based on life experiences, the other on faith. Although at first glance they seem to be at odds.

The church's theological virtues are faith, hope and charity. Charity is known as the greatest, it being a synonym for "love." Religion can benefit from what we therapists have learned about love on an intimate level, which is so difficult for many. Religions are good at instructing people to love "everybody," including their neighbors and God, but this is love from afar, which is easy. So, too, is writing a check to help the downtrodden, writing a spiritually uplifting piece or preaching a rousing sermon. But loving with continuum within the family, especially between the spouses, can be extremely difficult because of the psychological reality of "transference." (You'll read about transference in Chapter 10.) Transference is ever-present in all human relationships, especially marriages, and it can kill them. We shrinks are experts on it.

So religions can learn from us about intimate love and the barriers that prohibit it. On the other hand, as analysts, we don't spend any time with the virtues of faith and hope, and who in their right mind wouldn't want some of that? Many would benefit if religion and psychotherapy held hands as good friends.

When I became certified to practice on my own I did not shrug off my patients' religious beliefs. I found them to be psychoanalytically interesting and often revealing. As an analyst I was keenly interested in my patients' family dynamics and sometimes God and religion were part of those dynamics. (They certainly were in my house.) And I had noted that expressions implying family were frequently used in a religious context: God the *father*, holy *mother* the church; the blessed virgin *mother*, the *son* of God; *brothers and sisters* in Christ.

Most kids who learn about God (and religion) are taught about these concepts by their parents or older siblings before the age of seven. By that time unconscious minds are mostly formed. When I asked my patients to describe God I heard a wide range of attributes from loving to vengeful, from forgiving to tyrannical. The patients' concept of God, then, could give me greater insight into the people who taught them— the ones who contributed the most to the making of their emotional make-up.

As psychoanalysts we do not ponder the question of God's existence. We leave that to the theologians and philosophers. We struggle with tangible questions like: why are we so mean to each other, especially to family members who are closest to us? When there is a murder the first place the police look is within the deceased's family. They know from experience that family members kill each other more often than strangers kill strangers. Hell, the first murder recorded was a sibling rivalry between Cain and his brother Abel. Cain was convinced that God loved Abel more, so he killed him. Good grief.

I have a buddy, Tom, who doesn't go to church unless it's a wedding or a funeral. Tom and I walk our dogs together and one day I asked him (as I was writing this chapter) if he believed in God. Tom and I normally kept our conversations light, sports and politics, so this was unusual. He stopped walking, looked at me and said, "Yes." He paused for a few seconds and added, "You gotta believe in something."

I was surprised by his straightforward answer with no qualifying words and no waffling. I then asked him to describe God and he said,

"I can't describe him. All I know is he's the reason most people want to be good." I wish I'd said that.

Most people have a need for God to exist no matter their circumstances. Karen Armstrong, in her wonderful book *The History of God*, tells the story of Jews interred in a Nazi concentration camp. They decided to put God on trial for what he'd allowed to happen to them. The trial was held and they found God guilty as charged. But before they could pronounce sentencing, a bell rang. It was time for prayers.

I soon became comfortable with my given religion and my chosen profession. I witnessed much goodness emerge as my patients and I connected. By unleashing anger and discovering their individual truths, I helped their depressions lift and enabled creative juices to flow. Senses of humor showed themselves and bitterness abated as the abilities to love, and be loved, emerged. Good stuff that would make Jesus smile.

4

My First Patient

She Was Perfect

When my session on a Friday was over I got up and proceeded to the door of the consultation room. As I passed Jean's chair he handed me a piece of paper. He'd never done this and I asked what it was. It had a woman's name and phone number on it. "Call her and set up an appointment," he said, "she'll be your first patient."

I almost fainted. I had no inkling he was going to do this. "Are you sure I'm ready?" I asked, hardly believing I was really going to see a patient.

"You're more than ready."

"How do I set up an appointment?" I said, more to myself than him.

He looked at me like I was five years old and said, "See what openings we have at the front desk," and out the door he went, leaving me staring at the paper in my hand.

After I composed myself I called "Trisha," telling her I was Jim Joyce from the Institute for Child Development and Family Guidance. She responded in the chipperest of voices. "Oh, thank you for calling me back. I really do want to talk to someone. Will you be my doctor?"

Nobody had ever called me a doctor and I certainly didn't feel like one. The thought of a title never crossed my mind. I hesitated, then said, "I'll be the one seeing you. Please call me Jim." I then asked if it was urgent that she come in (in other words, was she suicidal?) and she said no—she just wanted to sort some things out in her head. "General stuff," she called it. She wasn't sure of the institute's location so I gave her directions.

"Thanks, Jim. I hope you're as nice in person as you sound on the telephone. When can we get together?"

We set up an appointment for the following Monday morning. When I hung up I noticed my heart was pounding and my palms were wet.

I'd been nervous before but never for such a duration. The weekend was a blur as I pored over my textbooks, unopened for at least a year. My ongoing training now was simply my ongoing personal analysis. But much of that was "boy" stuff and my first patient was a "girl." What did I know about girls? Nothing! And what did she mean by "general stuff?" I was a wreck.

Hx—Int—Res

On Monday morning I got to the institute an hour before Trisha's appointment and began drinking coffee, smoking cigarettes and pacing. In the back of my mind was the thought, actually a wish, that Trisha would not show up. She certainly didn't sound like she needed a shrink. She sounded happier than me.

I watched the first group of patients being greeted by their analysts and disappear down the hallway. It was inconceivable to me that soon I would join this elite group and would actually have a patient of my own. Then my stomach flipped as I had the thought: My God, what if I say the wrong thing? She's going to depend on me to help her and my every word will be scrutinized. And if I don't calm down she'll notice that I'm nervous and she'll think she caused it. What if she runs out of the building in tears?

With twenty minutes to go before her appointment I convinced myself that I had no business "seeing someone." With mounting panic I sought out my buddy, Richard Geer, a pediatrician and co-founder of the institute. Although primarily a medical doctor, he was psychoanalytically astute. (As a doctor of children he had a front row seat to observe the makings of future mental health patients.)

The institute was in the Mercy Hospital complex in Durango, and I walked as fast as I could to Dick's office. It took all of my willpower to not break into a sprint. Lucky for me he was between patients.

"Dick, I've got to see you," I said. He noted my anxious state.

"In there," he said, pointing the end of his pipe toward his office. "What's wrong?"

"I'm seeing my first patient in a few minutes, if she shows up, and I don't have a clue what to say. I don't know how to be a psychoanalyst. I'm still a patient!"

Dick grunted and told me to sit down. "You don't have to say anything. Here's what you do." He scribbled something on a prescription pad in his doctor's handwriting and gave it to me. "Hx—Int—Res." I stared at it, then asked, "What the hell does this mean?"

"Get the history. Interpret. Take to resolution. That's all there is to it. The first part should take at least six months."

I felt better. Asking Trisha questions about her past would be easy and I had six months to do this. The other stuff I could figure out later. I thanked him and left. (I carried that slip of paper in my wallet for many years until it fell apart.)

I rushed back to the institute. In the waiting room was an elderly couple and a beautiful thirty-something woman. "Jim," Rachel, the receptionist, said, "Trisha is here. She's your nine o'clock." I silently thanked Rachel for not saying "your first patient."

Trisha stood up, gave me a big smile, and we shook hands. "How do you dos" and "nice to meet yous," were exchanged. "After you," I said gesturing down the hallway. "The third door on the right."

I followed her down the hall and could not help but notice my patient had a very pretty rear end. "God, I'm still sick," I thought to myself. "I should not be psychoanalyst!"

She walked into the room and hesitated. "Am I supposed to lie on the couch or sit in a chair?"

"However you'd be most comfortable," I said, impressed with her openness.

"I'll take a chair for now," she said and seated herself. I took the other one.

She placed her tote bag on the floor beside the chair, crossed her legs and folded her hands in her lap. She was wearing moccasins, jeans, and a blue turtleneck under a suede vest. Her auburn hair was in a pony tail tied with a blue ribbon. There was a hint of lip gloss, subtle blush and hoop earrings. Colorado perfect. As she continued to smile at me it became obvious she wanted me to say something first. I knew I was supposed to wait for her to start talking, but the words popped out of my mouth: "How can I help you?"

She burst into tears.

Remembering that shrinks were not to interrupt crying, I passed her a Kleenex. She took it without looking up and continued to sob. My stomach flipped as I wondered what I was doing in that room. Then the terrible thought crossed my mind, "What if she never stops crying?" But she eventually composed herself, looked into my eyes and with the trust of a child said, "My life is a disaster. Will you help me?"

"Yes," I said, and held her gaze. It was the most sincere "yes" of my life and at that moment Trisha and I connected. It no longer mattered that she was a girl and I was a boy. We were fellow travelers through life … and I was fifteen chapters ahead of her.

"Tell me about yourself," I said, "and take your time. I want to know all about you." Her relief was palpable—and I realized what I was doing in that room.

I learned in our first hour Trisha had a Ph.D. in geology. She'd taught at a university in California for six years and had recently moved to Durango to "get my head on straight." Her verbal skills and intelligence level were superior. Listening to her talk was at once pleasurable and somewhat intimidating. She was smart!

I also learned in the first session that Trisha was twice divorced, practiced birth control, had a casual sex life, had committed adultery in both marriages, and had had an abortion. Currently she had "sworn off men."

"I can get myself off just fine and don't have to fix them breakfast," she said with a faint smile. Trisha had done it all and I was glad that I'd resolved my Catholic conscience dilemma.

We began meeting twice a week. In between our sessions I could think of practically nothing other than Trisha. Was I helping her? What did her last dream mean? Does she know she's my first patient? Should I tell her? Should I interpret her neurotic needs to please everyone or wait awhile? Am I talking too much? Am I talking enough? She didn't seem quite herself in the last session. Maybe I'm screwing up. I was preoccupied to the point of obsession with Trisha. After a couple of weeks I told Jean, who was supervising me, that I could not stop thinking about Trisha and her problems. She was ever present in my mind. He laughed.

Next Patient Is a Mess

"I know what you're going through, Jim. It's called 'the only patient syndrome.' It happens to every beginning analyst." He then handed me a piece of paper with a name and phone number.

"Here's your next patient. Call him and set an appointment."

All of a sudden Trisha no longer dominated my thoughts, except during our time together, thanks to "Don," my patient number two, who was a disaster. When he came for his first appointment one eye was closed and the other bulged out. Like a terrified one-eyed horse he frantically scanned the room looking for a reason to bolt. He could sit in the chair for only a few minutes and then paced. Lying on the couch was out of the question. The man was buzzing with anxiety.

But in between sessions I didn't worry about him. It was sort of like having children. When you only have one you worry constantly. When more show up you relax. Meanwhile, even without my worrying, my patients were getting better. Within three months Trisha's ambivalence was lessening and she began to make tentative plans for her future. Don's one eye was now completely open and the other one was back in its socket. I had noted with amazement the evolutions of this "evening out" of his eyes—and he could now go an entire session without pacing. This is when the miracle of psychoanalysis became clear to me. I had said very few words to either of them other than to ask questions. I let them talk, and talk, and talk ... and I listened. And they were getting better.

In time I would help them piece together their thoughts and feelings by pointing out seemingly unconnected elements from their lives and showing how they were connected. This would be the "Int" phase which would take the longest time and provide the lasting benefit from their analysis. But even without interpretations, the talking alone was enormously curative. It seemed ridiculous and just too simple.

The Gift

Naturally I discussed this with Jean. "Jim," he said, "think about it. Who in their right mind is going to listen to somebody for an entire hour without interruption, and at the same time show concern? And who would be silly or stupid enough to actually ask them questions— giving them even more to talk about? And who could listen to all that convoluted rambling without making comments, suggestions and judgments? That's what they pay us for—to listen to them. You're allowing them to cure themselves. That's a great gift."

He proceeded to say that the longer I kept my thoughts and observations to myself, the healthier they would become and the more receptive they'd be when I did open my mouth. He assured me I would know, intuitively, when it was time to interpret. "You're gaining their trust. They've never been able to trust anyone before. That's why they're here." Then he added that I was doing very well and to keep listening. "You have connected with Don and Trisha. Stay connected and they'll tell you everything you need to know to heal them." He handed me another piece of paper with a name and phone number on it.

Within a few months of seeing patients under supervision I began getting referrals. Trisha, Don and others began telling their friends about me and some of those friends called for appointments. And some of them told their friends who also called. My practice was filling up and finding supervision became a challenge. Less than a year after Trisha's first appointment a man I worked with as a condominium salesman called the institute and asked for an appointment. "I'd like to see either Dr. Rosenbaum or Jim Joyce."

I was a psychoanalyst.

5

It Is Not Academic

It's Empathetic

One of the first things we learned as psychoanalytic candidates was that a person's I.Q. (basic intelligence) and his or her emotional stability have nothing to do with each other. Some of the most emotionally wrecked people I saw had Mensa level I.Q.s. Some of the healthiest were barely able to squeak through high school. This confounding truth was an ongoing source of wonderment to me, as it is for all psychoanalysts.

Take medical doctors, for instance. To get through undergraduate pre-med with high enough grades and class ranking to get into medical school demands a genius I.Q. of 140 or better. But doctors, as a group, are no healthier, emotionally, than the people who work at the grocery store.

One of my doctor patients (we'll call him "Tom") came to see me in a heightened state of anxiety coupled with severe depression. He had been self-medicating, stealing drugs from the hospital and regularly shooting up. His presenting complaint was that his new wife had dumped him for a faith healer who had visited their church. Tom had both an M.D. and Ph.D. and specialized in microbiology at one of the nation's most respected research institutions. His craft enabled him to be the catalyst for future medical miracles, and losing his wife to a quack was destroying him.

When a patient is depressed one of the first things we analysts must know is if there had ever been a suicide attempt, or if suicide was now being considered. Tom readily admitted he was thinking of killing himself. An old wives' tale states that people who talk about suicide never do it. That is nonsense. Tom had my undivided attention.

33

The Mind and I

I began seeing Tom twice a day, including Saturdays and Sundays. This is most unusual but Tom was unusually depressed and anxious. After two weeks we were able to back down to once a day, still including the weekends, but after a month we achieved a standard schedule, three times per week.

During our first week together sessions mainly consisted of Tom crying out his words like a blubbering child. I could barely understand him. My only contribution was to let him cry, never interrupting and, when a Kleenex got too wet to be useful, to hand him a fresh one. He always stopped crying long enough to thank me.

In the second week of therapy, Tom was able to start talking without too many tears and was mostly coherent. My immediate interest was in learning about his wife. I knew that she could not be the cause of his emotional meltdown; spouses, alone, don't have that power. Psychoanalytically they are symbols from the distant past, but she was the obvious, and least threatening, place to start.

I learned that Tom was "Tina's" third husband. He was thirty-five, she was twenty-five. She had at least two failed suicide attempts that Tom knew of, one in each previous marriage. Her faith healer boyfriend had three other lovers. Tina had to share him with these other women. Tina, obviously, had some serious issues of her own. In layman's terms, she was nuts. But Tom, the medical doctor with the 160 I.Q., couldn't see it. He loved her.

When I asked Tom about his childhood he told me his father was a well-known orthopedic surgeon. He specialized in sports medicine and made an enormous amount of money. Prominent athletes sought him out while the NBA, NHL, and NFL picked up the tabs. Tom's father worked long hours. When he was home he doted on his wife but had no time for his children. He did not abuse them in any way but kept his distance. His passion was his work. "Your father is a saint," Tom's mother often said. "He is devoted to helping his patients." Tom remembered only one family vacation and, in the middle of it, his father had to return to work. A multi-million dollar baseball player had taken a fastball to the elbow, cracking a bone. The best doctor to fix it was Tom's dad. The story made national news.

Tom was fifth in line out of six children. His mother's days were spent carpooling them to innumerable functions. Her nights were spent with her husband. They dined together, not with the children. Tom remembered no kisses or hugs from either parent, but he thought of his childhood as close to idyllic. He had everything a kid could want—huge house with swimming pool on the grounds of a country club, with a yacht club five minutes away. His shirts had little alligators on them and he attended the best schools. As Tom and each of his siblings turned sixteen, they were presented with the keys to a new car. A family tradition.

While talking about his childhood I could feel Tom become defensive. He knew that we analysts look for miscues in patients' childhoods. When I told him his childhood did not sound so wonderful to me, from an emotional standpoint, he looked hurt and angry. I said there was nothing wrong with country clubs and swimming pools but there was something wrong with emotionally distant parents. "Wouldn't you have liked some hugs and kisses to go along with the new Corvette? In fact, if you had to choose, wouldn't you have taken the hugs and kisses instead of the Corvette?" I asked. "How about hugs, kisses and a five year old Dodge Dart?"

"I see what you mean," he smiled as his eyes found the floor. "Did I tell you my older sister tried to kill herself last month?" he asked quietly. We connected. The analysis had begun.

It took over a year before Tom came to the realization that his attraction to Tina was based on his neurotic need to rescue wounded people and heal them. Unconsciously he wanted to be a saint like his father, thereby earning his mother's devotion. He was finally able to separate his need to rescue, keeping it in the laboratory, and in his personal life find a real woman, not an emotionally insatiable child hidden in a woman's body. Tom, smart as he was, had been unable to "see" Tina; he could only see who she represented to his unconscious—the aloof mother. On the other hand, a guy who barely made it through high school could have had Tina's number immediately, silently declared her too flaky, and walked away.

The reality that the intellect and emotions have nothing to do with each other is important to remember for those contemplating therapy. When someone goes to a therapist, at the beginning of the first session she should ask him if he was ever a patient himself. If the answer is "no," she should get up and leave. That therapist should not be in the business. I could not be more serious. I don't care if the therapist is an M.D., a Ph.D., or a doctor of divinity. If he's never been a patient he should not be in the practice of psychotherapy.

He could have read every book on the topic of mental health. He could hold the chair in psychiatry or psychology at a major university. He could be published extensively, even be on the best seller list. He could be more famous than Amos but if he has not had the experience of being a patient, with the feelings and insights the process reveals, he cannot possibly understand the psychic dynamics of the unconscious mind. Without that understanding the dynamics of psychotherapy will not be available to him. His knowledge will be intellectual. That therapist, with all his degrees, will be inept. Psychotherapy is about re-experiencing feelings. Understanding the theories is an important part of a therapist's training, but they are worthless without personal analysis.

It goes like this. All of us find commonality on the emotional level. It is a matter of degrees. Within us we carry goodness, evil, fear, joy, frustration, hope, love, hate and guilt. We are saints on the one hand and sinners on the other. We are the soldier who jumps on the grenade to save his buddies, just as we are self-serving. We are the fireman who charges through the flames to save the old folks, as well as the woman secretly wishing for her parents' deaths to free up the big inheritance.

Know Thyself, Shrink

Human beings embody both good and evil on the emotional level. To understand how true this is, and how deeply this yin and yang of goodness and evil are embedded in us, we must, for a time, be a patient. If a therapist has not had that experience he will not be aware of and, therefore, will feel immune to the forces of his unconscious mind. This makes him especially naïve and quite possibly dangerous. No book, high academic degree, or series of lectures can take the place of being a patient in order to understand and recognize the depth, power, and conflicting forces present in the unconscious mind of everyone.

5. It's Not Academic: It's Empathetic

It is only in the regressed, dependent, vulnerable state of psychotherapy, where total trust and sometimes incredibly embarrassing honesty pour forth, that we become aware of the workings of our emotional system. The unconscious must be heard and, most importantly, *felt* if it is to be grasped. A psychotherapist must have a solid grasp of his own unconscious before he starts messing around with someone else's.

Popular books concerning emotional health can be misleading and should not be expected to make someone "better." Their value, rather, is as vehicles to get a person to a shrink if, after reading them, he thinks that's a good idea. If anyone recommends a book to improve an emotional state, that person is psychologically unaware. It is interesting to me how many therapists recommend books to their patients. (Smacks of a lack of confidence.) No book will make someone emotionally better, although it may initially appear to do so. But the result will be short-lived and soon the person will be right back where he started, maybe even worse. "That book didn't help me at all. I must really be screwed up!" Books concerning the emotional mind can be harmful, especially if the reader has unrealistic expectations of them.

Naturally I include this book in that assessment. From it you'll pick up jargon so you can talk like a shrink; you'll read about some interesting people and concepts, and you'll gain a heightened awareness of how the mind works on the emotional level, yours and everyone else's. You'll also know more about me than you'll want to know, but none of that will improve your emotional state.

Mental health is about how we feel on a day-to-day basis. It's about what we do, and what we don't allow ourselves to do; what we think, and what we don't allow ourselves to think; what we say, and what we don't allow ourselves to say. It's about how decently we treat other people, and how decently we treat ourselves. And if any of the above are out of sync, reading a book will not help. Nor will getting a Ph.D. in psychology. Books, lectures, and academic schooling are food for the intellect, but the intellect and the emotions are separated by oceans. Only an emotional experience will correct an emotional problem.

It used to be that psychiatric residencies included at least some psychotherapy training in their curriculums but, sadly, that is rarely the case today. The training is exclusively pharmaceutical based. One reason for this is that the medical profession relies heavily on insurance companies. In other words, keep the costs down. Therefore "talk therapy" is often discouraged in favor of medications which, it is assumed, cost less. However, an article in *The Economist* (April 16, 2006) entitled "Talk is Cheap" states differently.

"Robert De Rubeis of the University of Pennsylvania ... conducted the largest clinical trial ever designed to compare talk therapy with chemical anti-depressants. The result ... is that talking works as well as pills do. Indeed, it works better if you take into account the lower relapse rate."

For some mental conditions, such as schizophrenia and bipolar, medications are essential. They can also have much value in cases of severe depression. But drugs should always be used in conjunction with person to person, intimate talk therapy. The emotional mind is people oriented.

Newsweek magazine (February 6, 2006) published an article by Jay Neugeboren entitled "Meds Alone Couldn't Bring Robert Back." Jay interviewed hundreds of former mental patients, many who'd been hospitalized for over ten years, and were now recovered and leading full lives: doctors, lawyers, teachers, custodians, social workers. Jay asked them what made the difference: "Some pointed to new medications, some to old; some said they had found God; some attributed their transformation to a particular program, but no matter what else they named, they all—every last one—said that a key element was a relationship with a human being ... most of the time this human being was a professional ... who said, in effect, 'I believe in your ability to recover and I'm going to stay with you until you do.' That's what brought them back."

6

What It's Like
to Be a Shrink

A God-like Business

Many people think being a shrink is a mysterious, even glamorous, profession. It is, but only at cocktail parties. The day to day doing of it is hard work and often involves the elements of: fear (I hope she doesn't kill herself tonight): frustration (Why won't this idiot admit to the obvious): boredom (Is he going to tell that story again!) Yes, there are joyful moments when the patients "get it" and there is much gratification as their lives improve. But therapy is more fun for the patients than for their therapists. Certainly it is more interesting to them.

The causes of most mental illnesses are easily determined. Although patients' stories vary in intensity, the psychic dynamics they reveal are finite and can be categorized. Unfortunately we cannot say, "Okay, 'Stan,' here's the deal. You're a number five and here's what you must do about it." Stan must figure it out himself; all we can do is guide him. Even though we have ascertained the root of his problems, from perhaps the first session, it could take years to get him there and we must be very careful that we choose the right roads to that destination. That's not mysterious or glamorous. That's tedious. It is a mixture of art, science, empathy, understanding, and, of course, training and experience.

After a therapist is certified and licensed the first thing he needs to do is find an office. He will need a comfortable chair with an ottoman, because he'll be sitting all day and needs to keep his feet up to prevent circulatory problems over the years. He'll need a comfortable chair for his patients and a couch. Although the couch has lost favor with many therapists today, I highly recommend it. It must be situated so that patients cannot see the analyst when they are lying on it. This is important and is the main reason for it. We don't want our patients looking at us. It's too exhausting.

A psychoanalyst will typically see six to eight patients each day. They'll be telling him things about themselves which, to them, are extremely important. If the patients are looking at him and note he's less than enthusiastic about their stories they will tend to embellish them, thus making them less valid, or they'll take the opposite tack and clam up.

Some therapists take notes during sessions, which is distracting to the patients. Before long they'll get a feel for what the therapist thinks is important—"He's writing that down"—and this may cause them to edit what they say, disrupting the all-important free flowing of words. If the patients are on the couch they can't see notes being taken. (But you can bet they're listening for a pen scratching on paper.) I never took notes during a session. When patients say something with analytic significance I could not help but remember. It defines them (becomes them) in my mind. Forgetting their names would be possible, but not their psychoanalytic dynamics.

The couch is also a wonderful therapeutic tool because it enables the analyst to listen with the "third ear." (Theodor Reik coined this marvelous phrase.) Listening this way allows him to hear substance rather than individual words, making it easier to gather patterns of thought and behavior. I closed my eyes and propped my elbow on the arm of the chair resting my cheekbone on my fist. This posture helped me to concentrate on the patient's unconscious material as it threaded its way through the volume of words.

A person's psychic make-up is formed over time by numerous people and events somewhat like tributaries form a river. Let's say the patient is the Mississippi. The analyst needs to discover Horse Creek, which feeds into the Kankakee River, which feeds into the Des Plaines, which feeds into the Illinois, which feeds into him, forming his unconscious mindset. The patient did not begin life as a great river; he was a trickle. His "contributaries," so to speak, need to be discovered (and there will be many of them), those who formed the person he is today. It will be a lot easier for the analyst to recognize these tributaries if his patient is not staring at him.

So why not begin with the couch? Why bother with that other chair? Because to almost everyone the couch is scary. (It sure was for me.) For many patients too much control is lost too soon. A face-to-face rapport should be established first. It may take just a few sessions or dozens of them before the patient trusts enough to give up control, lie down, and reveal what's really on his mind.

Ideally a psychotherapist's office will be somewhat secluded from the world's view. Most people, understandably, are reluctant to let others know they are seeing a shrink. A secluded location is not always feasible, however, as many therapists work together in clinics, hospitals, and institutions where they share common expenses. As a patient seeing Jean Rosenbaum at the institute, where many therapists practiced, I waited with others in a reception room. One day I was appalled when one patient asked another, "How come you see a therapist?" The embarrassed patient didn't look up from her magazine and her face turned red. When I saw Jean I told him about the incident, thinking he'd be disgusted by this insensitivity. Instead he laughed and said, "It's always dangerous to ask people why they're seeing a therapist. They might tell you."

Many therapists work out of their homes, which has advantages. It is private for the patients, the therapist doesn't have to drive to work and it makes fiscal sense. There must be a separate entrance to the consultation room, however, or it's not a good idea. Patients should not be traipsing through the therapist's house observing how "ungodlike" he is.

Yes, "god-like" is what a therapist must be to his patients. They are not bringing their problems and heartaches to an equal human being. They are bringing them, in their minds, to someone very special who can relieve their burdens. And this is a heavy responsibility on the therapist, one he must take seriously. That is contrived but it is also important. Patients have been seriously messed up by "normal" people— normal in their experience. The therapist must be above normal to help them. If he steps off the pedestal they have erected, damage will have been done to their therapy. These are patients, not clients. Clients see lawyers and interior designers. Patients are hurting, and it is imperative not to wreck the doctor-patient relationship they need in their time of desperation.

The less patients know about the personal lives of their therapist, the better it is for them. They don't need that distraction and are not in therapy to learn about their therapist. Over time it becomes clear to the shrink that his patients could not care less about him as a person anyway, and that's the way it's supposed to be. Only the lessons learned from the experience should remain with the patients. Psychotherapy should never be confused with friendship.

Shut Up

The most tempting pitfall a shrink can succumb to is talking too much. Silence is unnerving to the inexperienced or insecure therapist who may begin filling the air with words. If there is a silence, let it be. It is the patient's hour and the patient's silence.

I once saw a young woman, "Meredith," a shoplifter, who was given a choice by the court: Either get psychotherapy or spend time in jail. She wisely chose therapy. She came into my office, sat down, glared at me and said, "I don't want to be here."

I asked, "Why not?" Her eyes went to the floor and she stared at it for fifty minutes. Not a word was uttered. I then said, "Your next appointment is Tuesday at 4 o'clock." She left.

Tuesday at 4 o'clock she returned to my office and said, "I don't want to be here because I think it's a waste of time."

I smiled and said, "It's your waste of time, not mine. I'm getting paid for it."

This made her giggle. "The last time I kept waiting for you to lecture me. Aren't you going to lecture me?"

"No," I answered, "I'm not the law, I'm a shrink." I then asked her to tell me anything she wanted to about herself, and that did it. For the next three months I couldn't shut Meredith up. Silence is a wonderful tool at the therapists' disposal. It signifies defenses and removing them is an important part of emotional healing. The silence says, "We're close to something important."

Candidness can also be a good tool. I had a male patient whose preoccupation during our sessions was how much money he was paying me and how he was not being helped. His real problems were overshadowed by this concern, and he was driving me nuts. No matter what question I asked him about himself he would segue back to the cost and worthlessness of his therapy. After one of these sessions was over, I said, "Time's up Bob."

He responded with, "Well, there's another hundred bucks wasted."

As it turned out I had a cancellation for my next hour and said, "Bob, I agree. So far you've wasted your money. We've gotten nowhere." I then added that I had the next hour open and told him I would agree to continue the session if he'd agree to waste another $100. He looked at me like I'd gone daft, thought about it for a few seconds, laughed, and agreed to the deal. About halfway through the next hour, Bob, recently married, told me he thought he was gay.

I learned a lesson from Bob. Some patients, at least at the beginning of analysis, need more than the standard allotment of fifty minutes. (Analysis is called "The Fifty Minute Hour.") It takes more time, for some, to work up the nerve to tell what's really on their minds. Bob's bitching about money, and his attempt to belittle me in the process, was simply a defense against what he thought was a terrible truth about himself. He was six months married to Rachel (I knew her—she was a knockout) and unable to have sex with her. Bob figured he had to be a homosexual.

"What types of men are you attracted to, Bob?" I asked.

He gave me an incredulous look and said, "I'm not attracted to men."

"Then why do you think you're gay?"

"Because I can't get it up anymore with Rachel and she's a beautiful woman! I was fine until we got married, but now nothing happens. She's going to leave me!"

"Let's talk about getting it up and being married, Bob," I said. The connect was made and the analysis began.

Being a shrink is hard work. He is not simply listening to patients

43

complain about their lives. He is listening with that "third ear" to their personal history, patterns of thought and behavior and to their preoccupations. He'll note their joys (if any), pains, loves, hates, fears, guilts, wants, don't wants and dreams. He is also noting slips of the tongue, which are most telling. He is forming a picture in his mind of his patients' unconscious mind. Sometimes I had the feeling I was herding rabbits or loading pigs. Just when I thought the last rabbit was going into the pen or the last pig was on his way up the ramp, a patient would say, "Did I ever tell you about the times my father beat up my mother?" Prior to this the patient had portrayed dad as the gentlest of men, a henpecked Walter Mitty. Back to the drawing board.

It's Unnatural

Loneliness is a downside to the profession. Although he spends his day with people—one right after another—a therapist cannot be himself. He becomes a creation in his patients' minds, a figment of their imaginations, a shifting non-entity fulfilling their needs. He cannot confide in them that he, too, has problems, unrealized goals and fears. He cannot go to the movies with them or invite them to stay for dinner. They can never be friends. His day is filled with pseudo relationships. This is necessary for his patients' well-being, but it is an odd, unnatural way to relate to people.

Colleague friends are very important to a shrink. He spends his days observing how logic, reason, intelligence and educational levels are not active ingredients in the emotional area of human minds. This phenomenon demands regular reinforcement from peers.

Money is another downside of the psychotherapy profession. One must make a living, but sometimes the patients will have financial setbacks. What if they lose their jobs? Does a therapist dump them until they can pay again? With that rejection they need therapy more than ever. Also, in difficult economic times therapeutic practices are some of the first ones hit. Practical problems become more pressing than neurotic ones, and seeing the shrink is put on hold. The problem of finances is a constant in the psychotherapy business. A colleague once theorized that the reason Freud worked into his eighties was that he needed the money.

Another negative of being a therapist is the day-to-day grind of dealing with human misery. The analyst should remain emotionally detached from his patients and their problems to maintain objectivity. At the same time if he does not genuinely care for them they will intuitively know it and they won't get better. It is a difficult balancing act—objectivity tempered by caring. I never had a patient that I did not eventually like as a person. They all had sweet spots, although some took a while to find.

I mentioned in the preface that psychoanalysis is a dangerous profession. This does not mean patients sometimes attack their therapists with guns, knives, or fists. I was never threatened by a patient in any physical way, but they do attack in ways so subtle that neither you, nor they, know it is happening. Their neuroses sometimes plug into your neuroses and you begin to have their symptoms. It is bizarre.

Patients Are Contagious

When Bob, who thought he was gay, and I finally got into his analysis we spent a great deal of time on his anger toward women, which was the underlying cause of his inability to have sex with his wife. Bob had deep, unresolved issues with important females in his life, particularly his older sisters, who teased him relentlessly.

One night I was unable to "perform," just like Bob. This had never happened to me, and I freaked out. Fortunately I was seeing Bob under supervision and quickly called the supervising analyst and made an appointment. She heard my story and asked me to relate the details of Bob's last session. In doing so I remembered that I, too, had a similar experience with women in my past and, obviously, had not completely worked through it. An insight accompanied the memory and my problem was gone as rapidly as it occurred.

The insight and memory had to do with seeing, at the impressionable age of ten, a soiled Kotex at a neighbor's house. I was told by an older boy, who lived there, what it was and where the blood came from. In a hushed tone he said, "I got four sisters and they bleed down there all the time" pointing to his crotch. "And that's the place you're supposed to put your pecker so they'll stop bleeding." This was a most frightening concept to a ten year old and I recalled thinking that where the blood came from was certainly not a place I wanted to put my pecker. I had forgotten this episode in my life until Bob jarred it loose with a similar experience in his childhood. He'd grown up in a household of women and remembered, "Bloody rags were all over the place. My sisters taunted me with them."

My neurotic reaction to Bob's story was more dramatic than most, but it illustrates one danger of being a therapist. No one is completely, thoroughly analyzed. He couldn't live that long. So we are vulnerable to our patients' problems. Usually they show up as mild malaise, boredom—or fantasizing about becoming a forest ranger. We empathize both consciously and unconsciously with their stories. We can't help it, we are human. To lessen this danger to ourselves it is important for a therapist to have a therapist, to take regular vacations, and to have shrinks as friends. Being a psychoanalyst can be harmful to your mental health if you are not prepared when your unconscious mind gets zinged by the unconscious minds of your patients.

Lastly there's the problem of the yips. Ideally patients are true analytic cases. They lie down on the couch three times a week for a few years and re-live their past, paying scant attention to the present. This doesn't happen often. Patients have crises and need to talk them out. Most crises are neurotic fears that don't come to pass but occasionally they are real. Hearing about these real crises, over time, can be contagious, causing the analyst to think: Does my spouse still love me, I mean really? Is my child's mysterious illness a passing virus or is it life threatening? Is the bump on my leg a muscle or a tumor? How about that new brown spot on my face, age spot or melanoma? Etc. Patients' fears can be contagious because you never know, you know? Sometimes their nuttiness isn't nutty, and their worst fears do come to pass, thus passing along the yips to their shrinks.

When I went into private practice, a psychoanalyst buddy and I took turns seeing each other on a twice-a-month basis. We passed the same $50 bill back and forth, taking turns being doctor and patient. This strategy worked great and kept us grounded.

Being a psychotherapist has many positive aspects, too. He is doing a lot of good and the world will be a little better place because of it. He is also his own boss choosing how, when and where he works. The study of the mind is a relatively new and interesting field and the literature is rich. There are numerous seminars, workshops, and lectures to attend to enhance knowledge and tweak skills. From time to time eccentric characters like Albert Ellis emerge with a different take on the subject of mental illness. This famous psychoanalyst, who lived to be 94, once stated: "All human beings are out of their fucking minds—every single one of them." There's lots of laughs to be had as a psychotherapist.

Another nice aspect to the profession is that colleagues will not take themselves too seriously. They wouldn't dare because they understand the multiple entanglements and layers of neurotic thought in every mind, including their own. They are, by and large, a neat group to associate with. Most I know are bright, interesting, interested and have self-effacing senses of humor.

I once had a particularly difficult case and shared the dynamics with a colleague while we attended a seminar. When I saw her some months later she asked how that patient was doing. I was having a bad day and blurted out, "The bastard's doing better than I am."

Without hesitation she said, "I hate it when that happens."

7

Making a Diagnosis

It's All About Age

The emotional system is subject to illness just as are the various parts of the body, but to isolate an emotional illness, and put a completely accurate label on it, is impossible. A bodily illness, on the other hand, may exist without interaction with another part of the body. Many cancers, if caught early, are isolated and can be surgically removed. Broken bones can be set and heal completely. Sprained muscles will, in time, heal themselves. But mental illness must be treated holistically. Whatever the presenting symptoms—depression, anxiety, sleeplessness, phantom pain, panic attacks, phobias—none will stand alone. But the therapist must state a diagnosis for the insurance companies who insist upon them and often pay the bills. So sometimes we have to wing it. Back in the good old days the diagnosis was always "anxiety condition," no matter the presenting symptoms. We did not want to label people for the rest of their lives with a specific illness. Now we must, although it's often misleading

The America Psychiatric Association publishes the *Diagnostic and Statistical Manual of Mental Disorders* (DSM). It's become the bible for diagnostic purposes and contains a dozen or so classifications with a sub listing of the symptoms. However, if you read the symptoms it becomes clear that few patients will match the classifications exactly. And for good reason. Emotional illnesses do not occur all at once, like measles, the flu or cracked ribs. Emotional illnesses are contracted in stages, as in ages, during our formative years, and they overlap. Nobody can have "just one."

7. Making a Diagnosis: It's All About Age

Human beings go through seven distinct stages of emotional development before the age of seven and each of these stages leaves a permanent imprint on their adult personalities—both good and bad. It is fun to observe them and anyone who has raised kids will recognize them. The seven stages follow—the ages are approximate. The positives and negatives are not all-inclusive.

1. Oral—From birth to eighteen months: everything about the mouth.
   Adult Positives: Be able to communicate clearly, to enjoy food, to sing, and write. Be able to put trust in others.
   Adult Negatives: Obesity, alcoholism, smoking addiction, eating disorders. Speaking at a barely audible level or, conversely, talking too loudly or too much.
2. Anal—From 18 months to three years: learning to control down below.
   Adult Positives: Being organized, in control, be efficient, able to make decisions and stick to them. Artistic.
   Adult Negatives: Being slovenly or obsessively neat; thinking in extremes—either black or white, good or bad, pretty or ugly. In other words, being unable to see the grays of life. Always being late for appointments, cheap, compulsive, hesitant and ambivalent. Overly controlling of self and others.
3. Phallic—Three years to five years: whoa! More stuff down below is discovered.
   Adult Positives: Be a leader, take reasonable risks, defend yourself and others, be accepting of life's challenges, and be able to share. Not fearful of competition.
   Adult Negatives: Be physically and verbally abusive to weaker people; arrogant, braggart, daredevil; believing winning is everything, being insensitive to the feelings of those around you. Always selling yourself.
4. Oedipal—Five to seven years: the parent of the opposite sex becomes the primary love object.
   Traditional literature does not include Oedipus as a phase of psychosexual development, merely referring to it as the Oedipal Conflict, but I do because it also informs the unconscious—big time! This phase will wane at about age 8 but will return with renewed intensity during puberty.
   Adult Positives: Be able to maintain a long lasting and intimate relationship with a member of the opposite sex.
   Adult Negative: Be unable to do so.
5. Latent—Age 7 to puberty: As the name implies, a cool down time when the previous stages are incorporated.

49

Adult Positives: Being emotionally balanced without extreme highs
and lows or pre-occupations and fixations.

Adult Negatives: Not balanced: fidgety, flighty, flakey.

6. Second Oedipus—Puberty: another attempt to seduce the parent of
the opposite sex. Adult positives and negatives are same as first
Oedipal conflict (Phase 4).

7. Genital—From puberty to death: most important love object is
someone of the opposite sex outside of your original family.

Adult Positives: A peaceful, fulfilling, non-competitive, long term
relationship with a person of the opposite sex.

Adult Negatives: Jealousy of or disdain for people not of your gender.

Any of the negatives above qualify as symptoms of emotional
problems. It then becomes a matter of degrees.

Note: Stages 5, 6 and 7 are determined by stages 1 through 4.

So rather than using diagnostic labels, another system to diagnose patients would be to use numbers, as in ages, the emotional ages of the patients. In a sense, to be emotionally ill is to be childish. For instance, a manic-depressive (now called bipolar) is a person who suffers from mood extremes from euphoria to despair. This is normal for a two year old but not an adult. A three year old lives in a delusional fantasy land of self-absorption, not unlike those with untreated schizophrenia.

A psychopath is a two year old: "When nobody's looking I'm going to bite my baby brother." A sociopath is four—"Stealing stuff is wrong if you get caught." Those who can't maintain friendships and those who can't stay married are five. Pouters are three. Depression is the four-year-old in the nursery school, off in the corner by himself, head down, not interacting with the other kids. On the outside he's in a stupor. Inside he's screaming, "I want my mom!" A pedophile is sexually attracted to children—just like children. He's between 4 and 5. You get the idea.

Because our dominant emotional traits, which we carry throughout our lives, have their beginnings in our formative years, each can be traced to a chronological age of emotional development and sometimes people get "stuck" at that emotional age (or ages). In other words, their adult personalities have retained childhood feelings and behavior, traits that should have been abandoned, and outgrown. The narcissist thinks he's somehow entitled. He learned of his "specialness" when he was four, but should have figured out that his entitlements were relative to his actions by the time he was seven. He never got to that eminently more rewarding stage of sharing. He's "stuck" at age four.

Pass It On

Neurosis is a term we hear often. It's a catch-all diagnosis and none of us are immune. We neurotics experience fears or guilts that have little or no basis in exterior reality. In other words, the fears and guilts are all in our heads. They are no less real to us, however, and may not only be debilitating but take many forms that initially seem unrelated. But nothing in the mind stands alone, and a goal of psychoanalysis is to discover these emotional connections. The patient does this by first connecting with another person, the analyst, who then helps him make his own connections with his emotions and demonstrate how they are connected to his past.

Neuroses may also manifest themselves in the body. Elusive pain, excessive perspiration, persistent diarrhea, constipation, headaches, stomach aches, racing heart, rashes, hypertension and ulcers often have neurotic causes. I have treated patients with all of those symptoms and, without addressing any of them directly, over time they mysteriously went away.

It has been known for centuries that the mind and body have a psychosomatic relationship. Experienced M.D.'s are aware that many of their patients are not physically ill. Although the symptoms are body-based their causes are psychological. An old saying with merit is: "If you don't talk your body will."

But a word of caution: If you have a physical symptom you should see a medical doctor before visiting a shrink. Chances are your headache is caused by the fact you hate your job, despise your spouse, are in the middle of bankruptcy, or lost someone dear. But you never know.

Our emotional make-up is in our unconscious minds. To change it we need help from another human being because our emotional systems were developed by interactions with other human beings when we were kids. One of the interesting aspects of this phenomenon is that parents tend to stifle their children at the same stages (ages) of personality development that they were stifled. They'll be doing it without conscious awareness, however.

When we get into late teens and early twenties we all agree on just how poorly we were raised by our parents and vow not to do the same to our kids. But we do. Let's say a man is a super tightwad and pack rat who only begrudgingly spends a nickel, just like his dad. From this personality defect we can infer that his toilet training (and his dad's) did not go smoothly. But when he has children he will err with his two year old. Chances are his offspring will be just like him, so tight they squeak, or just the opposite, spending money with abandon. He will create an "either/or" person as his kids pass through the anal phase. He can't help it. "We should do unto our children as was done unto us" is an unfortunate program on hard drive in our unconscious minds.

Parents raise their kids the same way they were raised, psychologically, because it's the only model they know. We live (and always have) in a world of jealously, hatred, indifference, pettiness, selfishness and greed. These are childish qualities that should have been outgrown. As a species we have been psychologically slow to mature. I'd say we are about four years old, the phallic stage. Whether between nations or within our own families we can't seem to quit fighting.

I had a friend who grew up in Brooklyn, fought in the Pacific Theater during World War II, became a Trappist monk for eighteen years, then rejoined the outside world as a diocesan priest. He agreed with me, once preaching on this very topic of emotional aging, saying that the church is an evolving institution and, in his opinion, was currently four years old. This upset many parishioners. The point he made was that the church was preoccupied by innumerable rules, regulations, trappings and ceremonies which obstructed its essence—teaching the messages of Christ. "There's nothing Christlike about a cathedral," he said, adding that the size and grandeur blinds us to Jesus' simple messages of love, simplicity and forgiveness. "We lost our way centuries ago and now we're stuck!"

Two year olds are my personal nemesis, the anal people. Their need to control others is their preoccupation—think like me, act like me, believe like me. They wear righteousness and narcissism as badges of honor. They are self-absorbed, unable to explore, or even listen to, the unfamiliar. Stop the growth!

Too bad for us we cannot construct our own emotional systems. That was done by others before we were aware enough to pay attention. Therefore, we can not un-depress ourselves any more than we can give ourselves depression. We can, however, take charge of our intellectual growth to become doctors, lawyers, scientists, and mathematicians. We can also consciously set out to be CEOs, senators, presidents, and popes. And if we work hard enough, are smart enough and get the proper breaks along the way, we can achieve these goals.

"Sheila" (age 22) got drunk and stole a motorcycle. A first time offense. She came to see me as ordered by the court. She was very talkative and in the first session informed me that she did not believe in psychotherapy and by the way, she also hated men. "They are all assholes," she said, looking me right in the eye. Sheila made me laugh.

But over time we connected and she told me of the numerous sexual encounters she endured from her two older brothers from the age of seven until she left home for college. "I told my parents about it but hey didn't believe me. My lying bastard brothers denied it and my parents believed them instead."

So Sheila was emotionally stuck at age seven, making it difficult, if not impossible, to have a healthy relationship with a man. We spent many painful sessions re-living those years of her life when her brothers took advantage of her. One day, after perhaps six months, she came to her session smiling and said, "Last night I thought of something. I have put my trust in you. I told you things I've never told anyone—yet you are a man. Maybe I was wrong about men. Maybe they're not all assholes." That's how analysis is supposed to work—re-live childhood to correct the harmful input, and replace it with the healthy.

Although it would be diagnostically sound to use ages rather than the often nebulous labels of the DSM, it is probably best if we don't. To tell a forty-five year old corporate executive with a compulsive personality (who's driving his family up the wall with his "rules") that he is a two year old would be insulting. Better to simply label him OCD, or whatever, and be done with it. Besides, whether we use names or ages for diagnostic purposes the psychotherapeutic approach will be the same: "Tell me about yourself."

The psychological community cannot take credit for discovering the importance of childhood on the human personality. One's family background was always a barometer of a person's character. Thus the expression: "He or she is from good stock" (not unlike a Hereford). In the eighteenth century, one hundred and fifty years prior to modern psychology, the concept acquired a sophisticated voice when English poet William Wordsworth simply stated, "The child is father of the man." In the nineteenth century William Ross Wallace wrote another profound truth, "The hand that rocks the cradle is the hand that rules the world." (How's that for pressure, folks?)

8

Sex and Sexuality

A Big Deal

Let me tell you about my pigs. You will recall I raised twelve of them: five were sows (female), six were barrows (neutered), and one remained a boar (male). When my first sow was ready to mate I herded her into the pen in the barn where the boar lived. The boar, a huge red-haired brute, nudged her and she nudged him back. She coyly went to the corner of the pen and looked back at him, and he slowly followed her bumping her sides and her rump with his huge snout. They exchanged playful nips and low grunts. This foreplay went on for many minutes before sexual intercourse began. It was amazing. He was a gentleman and she was a lady. Who knew?

When I went back to the barn to check on the pigs, they were lying together fast asleep, their huge bodies snuggled tight. They were snoring. The boar and sow had had two goals: to sexually satisfy themselves and their partner and to make little pigs. They had no ax to grind from the past (they'd just met) and they'd probably never see each other again. This made their sex act very simple. But human beings live together, raise kids together, have friends, neighbors, and intertwined families together and in doing so create a milieu of issues between them, all of which can cloud up the marriage bed. It doesn't take long for "having sex" to get complicated.

Another cloud over the marriage bed is the concept that having sexual intercourse is the ultimate expression of physical love. This puts a heavy burden on the couple to feel especially loving toward their partner when engaged in sex and is sometimes the source of much guilt.

Dozens of times patients would say in anguish, "I was having sex with my husband/wife but I was thinking about someone else! There must be something really wrong with me and my marriage." When I told them this fantasy was not an indicator of a bad marriage and was, in fact, quite normal, their relief was immediate. Happily married people have no reason to stray physically, but to stray via fantasy is simply being human. The ultimate expression of physical love may well be the holding of a spouse's head when she is vomiting, or changing a spouse's diaper when he's too old or sick to get out of bed.

We shrinks have been accused of being preoccupied by sex, and we are, but only because sex acts are symptomatic of what's going on in the unconscious. Sex acts, or lack of them, can reveal worlds of information about a person's psychic make-up and should never be neglected or glossed over in analysis. Sex is often, some say mostly, the main source of neuroses, but is, at first, unrecognizable as such. Sex is embarrassing for many people to talk about, especially concerning themselves, and we have to be very careful to not broach the topic too soon, lest we scare the patient off. But if a patient's sex life, including fantasies, has not been thoroughly analyzed then a complete analysis has not taken place. It's that important.

Once a solid rapport of trust has been established with the patient sex talk can begin. Sex acts are often thinly disguised in dreams, which gives an opening with reticent patients. Other patients, like my first one, "Trisha," are almost immediately forthcoming. Interestingly, I found that my women patients had an easier time talking about sex than the men.

Following are some typical "sex problems," and possible psychological causes of them. To get to the causes we ask questions, and if they are not on the mark they are in the area. Remember, sex acts are symbolic of deeper, more important, personality functioning. Following are some sexual dysfunctions and (in parentheses) the possible or probable causes beneath them.

> Excessive masturbation: Why are you anxious? What's the future hold for you? (The symbol is stopping time.)
> Premature ejaculation: Are you afraid of women? (The symbol is "Get me out of here!") (It could also symbolize anger at women—not waiting to give her pleasure.)

Unable to climax: Are you afraid to trust someone of the opposite sex? (The symbol is fear of being out of control.)

Dislike sex: What fears or guilts have you experienced after having sex? (Symbol is sex is dirty, sinful or shameful.)

Terrified of sex: Has anything bad happened to you regarding sex? (Symbol is sexual childhood abuse.)

Gigolo or nymphomaniac: Have you experienced more than your share of frustration in life, especially from your parent of the opposite sex? (Symbol is insatiable needs.)

One-night-stand specialists: What's your fear of getting to know someone as a person rather than only as a sex object? Is there something about you that you don't want anyone to find out? (Symbol is "Gotta go. See ya.")

Perpetual adulterers: What is your fear of making a total commitment to your spouse? What terrible thing would happen? (Symbol is keeping options open so you're not trapped.)

The answers to these questions, even if totally candid (this wouldn't happen), will not "cure" the patient of his dysfunction immediately. The questions and their answers merely get a dialogue started and allow the patient to settle into it. Because a part of his unconscious has been touched, if only lightly, he will be evasive and defensive and that's fine. Mainly the questions say: you have a sexual dysfunction; it does not stand alone; it is a symptom of something deeper within you and my interest is in that deeper you. The questions set the tone that the patient is much larger than his presenting problem. He already knows that and for the analyst to reaffirm it is a great relief to him, enhancing his ability to trust. The presenting problems will correct themselves over time as the trust and dialogue continue. In fact, they may never be mentioned again. But there'll be no shortcuts. It takes years to customize an unconscious mind. To think it can be changed in weeks or months is naive.

Let's Find Your Other Half

Another contributor to emotional problems is confusion regarding our "sexuality." The first and most important thing we learn about ourselves is: am I a boy or a girl? Thanks to Carl Jung, 1875–1961, the Swiss psychiatrist and psychoanalyst, we've learned the answer is "yes." Jung came up with a theory called "anima-animus" regarding the human psyche. Anima is female; animus is male. Jung discovered that we carry the emotional traits of both sexes within us. He knew, of course, that our biological genders were determined at conception but his research made him aware that our emotional genders did not always follow suit. Every person is both male and female emotionally. It is then a matter of "Who's in charge?"

You are familiar with the expression "the battle of the sexes." This battle actually begins within each individual: the little boy within scrambling for dominance over his little girl within, in the case of a male child, and vice versa in the case of a female. In most cases this battle is an easy one. If the proper role models are in place, ideally the natural parents who are not distant or seductive with their children, the battle is won without a shot being fired. But sometimes a gender role model is weak or missing, or a parent of the child's opposite sex ridicules or denigrates the child's biological gender, or sexually seduces the child. Then the battle is fierce.

In the model family there is a mom a dad and some kids. The girls take on their mom's personality traits and the boys take on dad's. But sometimes a boy will take on some of the mother's traits and the girls will do the same with the father. Ideally, the children will mostly identify with the parent of their own sex, but this identification will not be total, causing overlap. This is how it's supposed to be. Such identifications enrich individual personalities and the species. For example, I am mostly like my dad in my intolerance and quickness to anger, but I have a lot of my mom in me, too. I love to cook and don't mind watering the plants. My sister is mostly like our mom: nothing is more interesting to her than her children, but sometimes I see our dad come through in her when she's too generous for her own good. She can also fix the dishwasher.

No analysis would be complete without getting to understand "both sides" of the patient. It is always enlightening, and will produce emotional growth, especially when the subservient side is rediscovered and given room to blossom.

Male and female personality traits vary from culture to culture. In the U.S. culture (more a society than a culture), it is usually the man who will fix the car and the woman who will fix the dinner, but not always. The man is the predominant moneymaker while the woman augments his income. Dad cuts the grass, mom makes the beds. The husband is stoic in the presence of tragedy, the wife cries openly. Dad is distantly aware of his children's activities. Mom is intimately involved in them. These are generalizations, of course, and in any of these instances reversal of the roles is acceptable.

What is unacceptable in our society, and everybody else's, is a man going to work wearing a dress, nylons, and high heels. Or a woman sitting behind her desk wearing a suit, tie and wingtips while puffing a big cigar. Something's wrong: anima-animus is askew; it is also askew when people are sexually attracted to their own gender. Their personal battle of the sexes has been lost.

In Sex and Sexuality

Homosexuality is a phenomenon that has been part of mankind throughout the ages. Traditional psychoanalytic thought is that the stages of psychosexual development were mishandled by parents, culminating in a role reversal during Oedipus where the child identifies with the parent of the opposite sex, getting "stuck." On the other hand, biology may be the cause or, perhaps, it's a combination of nature and nurture. Nobody knows for sure.

Estimates land on about 10 percent for the number of people who are gay or lesbian. They did not cause or wish themselves to be so, nor can they change (or want to); to criticize or ridicule them shows ignorance, and, probably, fear of one's own sexuality. (Thou dost protest too much.) Being afraid of our "other side" is a common phenomenon.

Today, you couldn't count the number of books, articles and "how to" videos that soberly and intellectually address every conceivable aspect of sex. Advertisements for Viagra and Levitra, drugs which treat erectile dysfunction, are everywhere. One of the golf tournaments on the PGA Tour is the Levitra Western Open. Obviously there are millions of men who can't get an erection naturally. Before taking drugs they should see a shrink to determine if the cause is psychological. It many

cases it will be their fear of "their little girl within" whom they unconsciously transform into the woman they're in bed with. Paradoxically,
if they'd let the little girl blossom, she'll help them blossom. They'll not
become effeminate, which is the fear; they'll become more human.
(Okay, that's heavy, but so, too, is the power if the unconscious.)

Ours is a macho, "Ford Tough Truck" society that plays into the
fears of many men who believe that tenderness, intimacy and creativity
are for sissies only. What those men do not understand is that they are
being cheated out of expressing parts of themselves. Rocking babies,
baring the soul, tending the flower garden and being creative are not for
women only. These are human assets to be nurtured, not neglected,
feared or repressed.

We shrinks have been accused of starting the sexual revolution,
which began in the mid twentieth century. This isn't true. A case could
be made it was Irish writer James Joyce (no relation) who started the
sexual revolution, at least in modern literature. After the obscenity ban
on his novel *Ulysses* was lifted, other novelists piled on by filling up their
works with explicit sexual content. *Ulysses* has been acclaimed by many
scholars as the best novel of the twentieth century. If you have infinite
patience, and three Ph.D.'s, you may get through it, finding it at once
unbelievably brilliant, tedious and laden with sexual references.

Before the sexual revolution sex had been a taboo topic in film, but
now you can't see many movies or watch a television sitcom without
being inundated by it. We psychoanalysts not only didn't start the revolution; we don't support it either. We are as offended as you are. (Or
as you should be.) Sex in the city, and out in the country, is being triv-
ialized. It's de-humanizing. The goal of psychoanalysis is to enable people to love, work and create, not to prance around naked or have sex
with no commitment.

The sexual revolution can be attributed to many factors, including
Dr. John Rock's invention of the birth control pill, Vietnam (make love
not war) and, of course, *Playboy* magazine. *Playboy* took women's clothes
off, exposing their naked bodies to the world. Hugh Heffner, the magazine's creator, was rightfully accused of exploiting and demeaning
women. What I've never heard is how exploiting and demeaning his
magazine has been to men, and, in my opinion, more so. Who is it that

takes the magazine into the bathroom and locks the door? Heffner demeaned both sexes.

Sexual intercourse can be thrilling, fulfilling, rewarding, loving, giving, caring, joyful, playful, the most fun we can have and, at orgasm, the most pleasant physical sensation we are capable of experiencing. But sex can also be embarrassing, cruel, hateful, terrifying, painful, demeaning, degrading, demoralizing, dangerous and even deadly. It is a complicated issue with both of the good and the bad symbolically manifesting unconscious individual realities.

I saw a young couple, early 20s, for marriage counseling. She insisted. He was reluctant. Their sex prior to marriage was described as "just fine" by the wife and "great" by the husband. But shortly after the marriage it was described as "painful" by the wife and "even greater" by the husband. When love making began he started playfully, and softly, pinching his wife, but as things heated up the pinches got harder and by orgasm time (his), she was crying, "Stop it!" He thought she was becoming frigid ("like all married girls do"), claiming his pinching was always gentle, even when she showed him the marks on her body.

Obviously the husband had unconscious anger toward his wife (and as it turned out all women) and this anger showed itself during sex. The hurtful pinching was the symptom of his rage. When the subject of his anger toward women was broached he quit therapy and they soon got divorced. She continued therapy "so I won't wind up with another one like him." He, meanwhile, went prowling for his next victim.

There are many ways to learn about the unconscious but few are as telling as sexual behavior.

9

The History of You

HX

Carl Jung was a workaholic and unlike his wife he needed little sleep. After Emma Jung went to bed, Carl would sit in their darkened bedroom sipping cognac after cognac while thinking great thoughts. One night he began ruminating on the recent scientific discovery that from the moment of conception the microscopic body of a human fetus begins the millions-of-years' journey of mankind's evolution. While in the mother's womb the person will begin looking like an amoeba, evolve to look like a tadpole, then a lizard, a bird, a monkey, a Missing Link, a Neanderthal and finally a Homo Sapiens. This evolutionary process, when you stop to consider it, makes the saying "the miracle of birth" frivolous. The miracle occurs at conception and continues for the next nine months.

As Carl sat in the dark drinking and thinking, he was clobbered by this insight: if the human being experiences all of the phases of biological evolution during its nine months in the womb, it must also experience all the phases of psychological evolution. *"Zufluchsort scheiben sie!"* (Holy shit) he said to himself. He dashed into the bathroom, so as not to disturb Emma, turned on the light and began making notes.

This insight, which became known at the "bathroom insight," evolved into Jung's theory of the collective unconscious. It made the man famous and further study proved him to be correct. There are primitive symbols, he called them archetypes, that mean the same thing to all people, no matter their culture or where they live.

But there was little value to this discovery from a therapeutic standpoint. Unlike Jung's anima-animus insight, which could clearly be demonstrated to patients and corrective adjustments made, if appropriate, the collective unconscious theory couldn't really be "used" in therapy. It is mostly fun information to have and dispense. (Sometimes you dream you can fly like a bird? Guess what, you used to be like a bird.)

Although our emotional evolutionary history begins in the womb we will have no conscious memory of our time there, so we won't be able to talk about it. I had patients claiming they remembered being born, but I didn't believe them, and even if their memories had been accurate they'd have little to do with the ensuing events which caused their adult neuroses. And, no, I did not tell them I did not believe them. I simply said what every shrink says when he doesn't know what else to say: "That's interesting."

Psychoanalysis begins with the patients talking and the shrink listening and, from time to time, asking a question. If all goes according to Hoyle, that is also how it ends, years later. You have heard people say, in an attempt to sound wise, "I have never learned anything while I was the one doing the talking." That is a stupid statement. By listening to our words we discover how much we know, and don't know, about a topic and how much we are learning as concepts either come together or fall apart. Nowhere is this more evident that when we are talking about ourselves to a person who has been trained to listen with that "third ear," picking up our patterns.

The therapist listens, then uses questions to function as mirrors to our words. Now we will not only hear them but will see them or, more accurately, see the images, scenes and dynamics that the words describe. We can learn worlds about ourselves by talking about ourselves and sometimes this mirror will bring us to an "insight"—a crystal clear truth which heretofore had been hidden in the dark. These are thrilling moments for the patients and their therapists. Once an insight has been experienced it can no longer remain hidden. It is a truth and when enough of these truths are uncovered, the patient's mental illness will be on the run. It is marvelous to observe and it all comes about from … talking.

An example of an insight is the following: "Patricia" was twenty-seven years old. She came to see me after a failed suicide attempt. In our first session she said, "I'm just like my mother. We are two peas in a pod."

"How so?" I asked.

"There are so many ways I can't begin to tell you."

"What are some of them?"

"We look alike, although I'm tall like my dad. We love to shop. We like to lay out in the sun. We like to take trips. Oh, everything."

"How else are you like her?"

"Oh, millions of ways but I just can't think of anymore now. Everybody has always said I'm just like my mother."

"What's your dad like?" I asked.

"He'd never go shopping," she laughed. "He thinks sun bathing is a boring waste of time. His idea of a good time is staying home to work in his garden. My mother hates insects and dirt so I always helped Dad with the garden. He's very moody, sort of like me. He takes antidepressants—the same ones I do. And he drinks too much but who am I to criticize? Mom never drinks. And once, when he was younger, he also tried to kill himself. That's a secret."

"What's his name?"

"Patrick. I was named after him." After a long pause she said in amazement, "My God, Jim, I am much more like my dad than my mom! No wonder I'm so screwed up!" Patricia just had an insight.

Unfortunately all patients do not have the same capacity for insight. In fact, some patients are completely devoid of it. You can hold the word mirror right in front of their noses and they still don't get it. In these cases the shrink has a lot more work to do, as he must now resort to using "interpretations" for the patients to learn what's important about their pasts.

A typical interpretation would be one that I gave "Sharon." She'd come to see me because no matter how hard she tried, she could not keep a boyfriend. She'd been through dozens of them and the relationship with her current beau was beginning to sour. She wanted me to help her hang on to him. After getting a general history I made the following interpretation: "Sharon," I said, "your inability to have a relationship with a guy for more than a few months appears, at first glance, you are unable to commit yourself to just one person over the long haul, or the guys you choose are unable to do that. It probably is both. I think this is because you were much more devastated when your parents got divorced than you care to admit. You were only twelve years old when your father left. So let's forget about your current boyfriend, we both know he'll soon be a goner anyway, and talk about your parents' divorce. Please do not leave out any detail, as it may be the key to your relationship problems."

This interpretation by me was not as effective as if Sharon had put it together herself, with her own insight, but it got her into the proper arena of memory. It also implied that I expected to hear much pain when she returned to that terrible time when her parents split up. It would be okay, then, for her to "let go," and to Sharon's credit, she was unable to stifle a laugh when I slipped in the part about the current boyfriend "soon being a goner."

I believe one insight is worth fifty interpretations. Most analyses are combinations of insights and interpretations, however, with the insights getting more frequent as time goes by. Once the defensive armor is cracked it is easier for the patient to get at the truth rather than having the therapist dragging it out piece by piece.

In our minds we all carry "truths" about ourselves that are not to be messed with by anybody, including a shrink. They are inviolable and untouchable. I had one such truth and I carried it like a badge of honor. It had to do with my only brother.

Bob is eight years older than me. When I began first grade he was a freshman in high school. He was a straight "A" student. His I.Q. was above the genius level. He had a singing voice worthy of the Metropolitan Opera. He could out-dance John Travolta. He played the piano and the guitar by ear. He was an artist, a poet and religiously devout. But that's not all.

My brother was a rock-solid 6'2" tall, an excellent tennis player and could knock the cover off a baseball. As a pitcher, his curve, slider, sinker, and fastball were superb. Once I saw him hit a single, double, triple and homer in the same game. No little kid was prouder of his big brother.

Early on my parents noticed that I (Little Jimmy) was probably not going to be a straight "A" student. I recall my horror at being tested during second grade for being "slow." So as far back as I can recall my parents often told me, "Don't try to be another Bob. Just be a 'First Jim.'" These were nice, comforting words to live by and naturally I carried them with pride into my analysis as proof of two things: (1) I came from two of the most understanding parents one could have and (2) My parents were far better than my wife's parents. Remember, my analysis began with marriage counseling, so there was competition between us regarding who had the best upbringing.

When I smugly told my analyst about these wonderful words of counsel from my parents he looked at me and said, "What they actually said to you, Jim, was that you weren't good enough to be another Bob." My chin hit my chest. He went on to say, "He's better than you'll ever be in the arts, school, music, religion and even sports. Where was this 'First Jim' supposed to show himself?"

This is an example of an interpretation and it was a tough one to swallow. I had been living on those seemingly kind words of my folks which, in reality, had given me every excuse in the world to be mediocre. And mediocre I was. I graduated from college, for instance, with a slew of C's, a couple of D's, and a few B's. Good enough for me and good enough for my parents. At least I graduated. Now I'm told by a psycho-analyst that those kind and thoughtful words of my parents were really a message to program me as average. Their words could have been, "You'll never be as good as Bob so no sense trying." I was flabbergasted by this simple truth.

Parents can be limiting, as well as limited. My folks, both from psy-chologically unsophisticated origins, had two essentially perfect children, my brother the multi-talented genius, and my sister, the saint. (My sister is seven years older than me.) So when I came along as a surprise, mom was forty, they did not know what to "do" with me. They certainly didn't "deserve" to have two geniuses, or two saints, so the surprise kid they decided to make average. My parents did not sit down and discuss this, by the way, and they'd be appalled and hurt if they were alive to read these words. My parents' "decision" to raise an average kid was worked out, separately, in their unconscious minds.

Analysts see a lot of this "limiting parent" syndrome. One or two kids will get the lion's share of attention and direction as the parents' hopes and dreams are invested in them. The rest of the kids get caretaking. This does not mean all the kids will not be loved equally, however. I certainly felt loved the same as Mary and Bob but I did not feel "invested in."

It took a while for my analyst's interpretation to take hold. He had shattered a thirty-year myth but take hold it did, and when I was accepted into training at the institute I made the effort to excel not only as a training analyst, under supervision, but also with the academic curricula. I found my niche in the Jewish science (my brother doesn't know beans about the id) but that's enough about me.

A patient's personal history is the crux of psychoanalysis. What people have "been through" mightily determines who they are today. But the most important parts of their history are those early years when their concept of "self" began to take shape. It's said that by age seven our personalities are set in concrete. In my experience we are not fully developed emotionally until after the second Oedipal Conflict—about age fifteen. Whatever the truth, analysts all agree our emotional system is locked in when we are young. So if someone sees a therapist he should be prepared to spend lots of time in his youth. That can be difficult because time, teamed with pain, fear, and guilt, can greatly distort memory. We analysts often hear patients say, defensively, "I had an idyllic childhood!"

"So how come," we say to ourselves, "you are now, and always have been, so miserable? You can't laugh, you can't keep friends, and you're sure the world is out to get you." Idyllic childhoods do not produce miserable people.

A Saintly Seducer

One of my patients, "Theresa" (29), had gone into a deep funk because of a failing one-year-old marriage. She told me at the end of our first session that, no matter what, I would not destroy the memory of her wonderful father who was now deceased. I told her I was not in the business of destroying wonderful memories (not necessarily true) and we'd just see how her analysis evolved. "My mother was a stone bitch but my father was a great man," she told me with a defiant look as she left my office.

The Mind and I

As the analysis progressed she began to have memories of this great man spending an awful lot of time bathing her as a child. This ritual evolved into her and her father taking showers together. This didn't end until she was well into puberty—when the stone bitch mother told wonderful father to knock it off. Theresa had no specific memories of herself and her dad in the shower. I asked Theresa if her dad washed her. She couldn't remember nor could she remember if she washed him. "What did his genitals look like?" I asked.

"I don't know," she answered.

"How would you not know if you showered with him? You were thirteen years old when the showers ended."

"Oh," she said, "I guess I must have seen him naked but I really don't remember and I'd never thought about that. It's curious isn't it? I must have seen him but I don't remember."

Theresa had male and female siblings but dad ignored them in favor of her. In a psychological sense he "married" her and if mom hadn't put her foot down on those showers there's no telling where their relationship would have wound up. Dad had been seducing his daughter and eventually Theresa began to realize this. As her anger at him flared her depression lifted and her marriage began turning around as the "saint" was seen for what he was ... most un-saintly.

It is inappropriate for children to see the parent of the opposite sex naked. To them the jungle-covered mysteries between adults' legs, mom's breasts or that huge (to them) penis of dad's are sources of bewilderment and fright for their little minds. Nudists who have the skewered notion that "all natural" is part of God's plan for human societies have it wrong. Exposed adult genitalia is far too confusing for kids. "Au naturel" has not been psychologically healthy since Adam and Eve (here they are again) became embarrassed and donned fig leaves to cover their private parts.

What about the primitive tribes who live in the remote jungles and rain forests of the world? They all walk around naked. That is correct and the operative word is "primitive." Sociologically and emotionally they pre-date Adam and Eve. After Adam and Eve were thrown out of paradise they tilled the land, becoming farmers. The primitives are still eating grub worms and pythons for breakfast.

10

Transference

Don't I Know You from Someplace?

Like so many of the psychic forces that affect our lives, transference takes place at the unconscious level. (I'll bet you're not surprised.) But unlike most other unconscious forces, transference is cool because it's easy to observe once we grasp the concept, and witness the abundant evidence. It is also a key ingredient of the psychotherapeutic experience. It is true that patients' personal histories are the crux of psychotherapy, but if they tell their stories without the presence of transference they will not be healed. Transference is fun to observe in everyday life as you catch yourself transferring onto others and being transferred upon. (Just pay attention.)

In a nutshell, transference means "everybody you meet reminds you of someone you've met before. I know how nutty that sounds but bear with me. We humans are a collection of accumulated experiences going all the way back to childhood when we began to meet people—Mom, Dad, siblings, other relatives, friends, neighbors, teachers, shopkeepers, coaches, clergy, etc. Add to this the numerous people we meet as adults, including those on television, the radio, in movies and in literature. All of these people, especially ones met early, will color future relationships.

When we meet someone new, our experiences with that "kind" of person prompts us to immediately begin making judgments about him or her. Acting like a computer, our mind begins collating stored data from our pasts and he, or she, will "re-mind" us of someone else.

The Mind and I

There are dozens of features about a person that will spark transference, such as gender, age, name, body structure, facial structure, skin color, eye color, hairstyle, smile, clothing, ethnic appearance, and where they're from. (For instance, everybody knows New Yorkers are stereotyped as obnoxious. If you've lived out West you know Texans are, too.)

Other, not so obvious, triggers will be smell, size and shape of the hands, sound of voice, jewelry worn (or not), over-all projection of self esteem (or lack of). Also contributing to transference will be the environment in which we meet a person such as in church, on a ranch, at a bar, at a baseball game, a PTA meeting, in prison, wherever. Learning a person's occupation will strongly contribute to the transference. By the way, transference is not *projection*. With transference we ascribe the attributes of others onto someone. With projection we ascribe our own. But I'm being picky. That won't be on the test.

I had a male patient, "Frank," who told me he was first attracted to his wife because of her smile. "Her teeth and lips were exactly like my favorite aunt's," he said. Frank fell in love with his wife the moment they met, immediately transferring all sorts of attributes to her that were like his aunt's. As he learned over time few were accurate, but then it was too late. They'd gotten married, had two kids, and now wanted a divorce. This situation happens often. You know the old saying, "First impressions are lasting impressions." Fewer old sayings are more accurate because of the phenomenon of transference.

Another old expression is: "The things you say when you're drunk are what you really mean." This may be correct in some instances, when the booze has just begun to act, but if you are really hammered and say things to a loved one that is hurtful, transference is probably the culprit. This is especially true when married people harangue each other while under the influence of alcohol. Because marriage is the ultimate transference relationship, those hurtful, hateful things that you really didn't mean, and are so sorry about later, were most likely things you wanted to say years ago to your parents of the opposite sex. The booze weakened your ego, the person you are today, and you wound up in a regressed, childlike state saying things to a spouse you never could have said to a parent ... but wanted to. (Getting drunk is called regression in the service of the ego. Just so you know.)

10. Transference: Don't I Know You from Someplace?

Transference is not limited to individuals, it is also at the core of group prejudice. I once heard a Jesuit speak at a Jewish Temple in Columbus, Georgia, on the topic of Christian prejudice toward Jews throughout two millennia. "Wherever Jews settled they were ridiculed and persecuted by Christians. "Why?" the Jesuit asked. "There've been lots of reasons posited but none strong enough to justify a wholesale slaughter like the holocaust."

He continued, "My theory," said the Jesuit, "is a phenomenon psychoanalysts called transference. We Christians are taught, make that mandated, to emulate the life of Jesus. Forgiving enemies, loving neighbors like ourselves, shedding worldly possessions and sacrificing whatever to help our fellow man, this is impossible for us mere mortals to do and it unconsciously enrages us. We'll never measure up. We'll never be real Christians!"

But there's no way we can consciously be enraged at the Son of God. We'd go to hell! So we take that rage, sublimate it, then let it re-emerge with a vengeance by transferring it onto Jesus' people, the Jews.

If there was ever a Doubting Thomas about the existence of transference, all Thomas would have to do is be a fly on the wall of an analytic session. He would hear the patient ascribe to the analyst (who naturally becomes a parental figure) all manner of beliefs, thought processes, wisdom and experiences that often do not apply. In most cases, where the sex of the analyst and analysand are different, Thomas would witness the analysand "fall in love" with the therapist. (This sometimes happens when analyst and analsand are the same gender, also.) It never ceased to amaze me how much patients thought they knew about me due to the transference. They certainly didn't know enough to fall in love with me, but that happened almost every time as they transferred feelings for a significant person from their past onto me. Transference, therefore, from a psychotherapy standpoint is not to be discouraged.

Knowing that my patients' love for me had nothing to do with me gave me objective knowledge of their needs, wants, fears and hopes so I could better do my job creating a picture of their unconscious minds. The patients resurrected their flawed "love object" from the past and placed that creation onto me, making me someone else, someone from their early years who had not done the job properly. I became a "wished for" parent. To them I was no longer their analyst, I had become their mom or dad (it could shift back and forth), and with this dynamic in place much of the early damage could be worked through and corrected.

It could be corrected because they transferred me into one of their parents. But I did not respond to them as that person had responded. I was responding as that person should have responded so many years ago. By making me into someone else, they underwent what's called a "corrective emotional experience." This second time around they got it right. The patients now received the "new" mom or dad's undivided attention, concern, and empathy. (The fact they are paying for this per-ceived love does not, curiously, screw up the process.)

Patients must make the shrink a transference figure if they are to get better, but they don't have to work at it. It will happen naturally and it matters not if patients and therapist are of the same or opposite sex. Transference is the single most important aspect of psychotherapy, yet some mental health workers discourage it. These are the same people who call their patients "clients." They are counselors, not psychothera-pists. O'Douls versus Guinness Stout. They should be shot.

Properly conducted psychoanalysis works wonders between same or different genders but I believe the ideal situation is when the therapist and patient are not the same gender. This dynamic is a natural re-creation of the Oedipal Conflict, that final phase of personality devel-opment which is the source of much emotional illness. The early analysts in Europe believed all mental illness stemmed from Oedipal problems. Oedipus, if you have forgotten your mythology, unknowingly killed his father and wound up, unknowingly, marrying his mother.

The Oedipal conflict shows itself when children, around age five, become enamored with their parent of the opposite sex and a mini-sexual attraction accompanies it. This is a natural part of the process of growing emotionally. The way parents are supposed to handle this is to gently, but firmly, push the child away from themselves and back to the parent of the same sex who is the proper one to identify with. On paper this sounds easy, but most parents mess it up, either by giving in to the child's wishes or by being too harsh in rebuffing the child's overtures.

I have a theory that the reason so many marriages fall apart after seven years (the seven year itch) is because parents can't handle the reverse of Oedipus which is also present. Their child is in the Oedipal stage of development and getting "feelings" toward the parent of the opposite sex but so, too, is the parent getting "feelings" toward their son or daughter. As horrible and inconceivable as that sounds, those feelings are present. Most parents are unaware this is natural and consider the feelings, and the thoughts that accompany them, to be abominable. These feelings, I believe, can break up a marriage. Unfortunately no one told parents it's natural to see and appreciate the sexuality and sensuality of their children and to understand the accompanying thoughts. What is abominable is if they are acted upon. The terror of succumbing to their base desires becomes too overwhelming so the parent splits, making up a bunch of socially acceptable reasons and being only vaguely aware of why he, or she, really wanted out of the marriage.

Oedipus, like so many psychoanalytic principals, sounds like total nonsense to most people and that is understandable. Feelings and their associated thoughts that are in our unconscious minds frequently defy logic, reason, common sense, and goodness itself. They call into question religious teachings and morality. Nonetheless they are present and no one is immune from them. Let me tell you a story.

Our house had always been a magnet for our sons' friends. They knew I was a shrink, and as they got into their teens they sometimes asked me to listen to one of their "really weird" dreams. I was happy to do this, being careful to comment on only the least embarrassing parts of the dream. Almost all of their dreams were loaded with Oedipal material.

One time "Ted" told me a dream which ended with him and a movie star standing a the edge of the Grand Canyon. They were holding hands, obviously lovers or soon to be. The movie star's initials were the same as Ted's mother's, which never occurred to Ted. He asked me to interpret the dream. I told him it was a standard, very normal Oedipal dream and pointed out that the initials were his mother's. "It doesn't mean I am going to marry a movie star?" he asked.

"Sorry, Ted," I replied.

Ted, my sons Alex and Zack and two other teenagers left the house and drove to Atlanta. Later Alex told me what happened. In the car they talked about the dream and Ted said that he thought I was a smart man, but I sure was wrong about all that Oedipal crap. There were a few seconds of silence and then Ted, thinking he was changing the subject, said, "You guys know that new kid in school, Tom Dean? Have you seen his mother? She sure is a hotty!" The other kids howled with laughter.

A male shrink and female patient, or vice versa, is probably the ideal to correct the patient's Oedipal problems (the stage is set), and like the relationship between parent and child the love between therapist and patient can indeed go both ways. Therapists do sometimes "fall in love" with their patients via the phenomenon of "counter transference." Like a wise parent the therapist must never act out sexually or seductively with a patient. If he does so, he should be put into prison, charged with two offenses: Sexual abuse and fraud.

I am serious, prison. To violate a patient's trust, even though the patient may have initiated the desire for sex, is to violate the entire psychotherapeutic process and to make fraudulent use of the transference. This is a mortal sin but I am sorry to say that, like incest, it happens a lot. The long lasting effects on patients is devastating. If a patient is a victim of sexual activity from a therapist, he or she should call the police. If the therapist did it to them, he (or she) will be doing it to others.

Counter transference is a constant, potential problem in psychotherapy because therapists are human and some patients will strike their fancies—big time. Patients become trusting, open and vulnerable, like children, and the temptation to do more for them than merely listening and guiding can be great especially if there is a physical attraction coupled with an unconscious "click" reminding us of someone else. Then it's an "uh, oh" situation and therapy for the therapist is called for. We can easily forget that if we were not placed on the artificial pedestal by the patient, he or she would not be so childlike and trusting toward us becoming so "lovable."

Negative transferences and counter transferences can also show themselves. They, too, call for therapists to get therapy if they can't rapidly work through them without help. "Who does this patient remind me of?" is a question all therapists should ask themselves from the start.

When a patient of the opposite sex discusses sexual needs, activities and fantasies, the therapist is listening with that "third ear" and sensuality, which would normally be present, is not. The atmosphere is best described as professionally friendly. In thirty years as a psychoanalyst I was sexually turned on by patients only twice. Both times I got blindsided.

Durango is a small town. After a few years of practicing it was impossible for me to go to a restaurant, grocery store, church or tavern without encountering a patient. In the years between my marriages I frequented a bar called the Solid Muldoon. One night I was approached by a woman patient whom I had seen earlier that day. It was her first session.

She had been sitting at the bar with another young woman. Both, by the way, were very attractive. She came over to my table and sat down next to me, and said, "Our session today was great. I feel so much better already. I wanted to do something special for you." She told me that she and her girlfriend decided they'd rent a room at the General Palmer House Hotel next door, take me with them and "show you the time of your life." I was blindsided. I thanked her for the offer, told her I couldn't do that and would explain why not at our next session. She laughed and said, "If you change your mind let us know," and went back to the bar. I watched the baseball game on TV until things settled down and got the hell out of there. Don't ask me who was playing.

Culture Shock

On another occasion I came out of a session with "Sylvia," another very attractive patient. She was from a foreign country with a very different culture than ours. This had been our fourth session. She had been resistant to therapy and the candidness and intimacy that is necessary for it, but during this session she began to let her defenses down, and I felt good about her new-found trust. As I was standing at the counter putting her next appointment in the logbook she came up behind me and tapped me on the shoulder. I turned around and she put her arms around my neck and thrust her pelvis into mine. She had taken her top off and was not wearing a bra. "Let's go back to that couch of yours," she said.

Shocked, I put my hands on her shoulders and gently, but firmly, pushed her away. "Sylvia, we can't do this," I said, "please put your top back on." I turned around to give her privacy and she left the building, slamming the door behind her.

I doubted she'd be back for the next session but I was wrong. She marched in and sat down, angry and sullen. She told me I had insulted her. I explained to her about transference and counter-transference and told her I simply couldn't have sex with a patient. It was the biggest taboo in my profession. She glared at me. I then segued into talking about morality, specifically adultery. She was married. She continued to glare, making me feel foolish. Although the words I said were correct, their effect was terribly lame.

"Our time together will not continue," she finally said with a touch of sadness. "If we do not make love, I cannot be intimate with you on the spiritual level and not the physical. It is my culture."

"But you are married," I said. "What does your culture say about cheating on your spouse? In my culture, my religion, that's a sin."

"The only sin is allowing your spouse to know about it. Then he is hurt. Hurting someone's feelings is a sin. If no one knows about it, no one is hurt and there is no sin." Her tone now soft. Her eyes sincere. "Come to me," she said and held out her arms.

The thought of making love to this beautiful, mysterious woman beckoning to me caused the clinical barriers of psychotherapy to fly out the window. We were now a man and a woman. I thought about making some Oedipal interpretation about her wish to make love to her father, that I was his replacement, but that would have sounded even dumber than what I had already said. I was not going to her nor was I terminating the session. She was now making the rules. I had lost control of our time together.

"I'm sorry, Sylvia, as much as I would like to make love to you, and I really would, my culture, religion and profession forbids it."

"Then we both lose," she said and walked out of my office, gently closing the door.

Shortly after this I heard that her marriage ended. I thought of calling her but another rule of therapy prohibited that: "Once a patient—always a patient." (Nuts.) I never saw her again but I've thought about her, both psychoanalytically and in other ways. Yes, therapists are human.

10. Transference: Don't I Know You from Someplace?

During our final session, after four years of in-depth analysis, "Janet" asked a question which I'd never heard before. "Tell me, Jim, what really cured me. Psychoanalysis or your love for me?"

This is another example of transference. I did not love Janet. True, I was fond of her and she felt that. But her concept of my emotional attachment to her far exceeded reality. In her mind I had become the loving father she never had. She needed that dynamic to make her well and her question was rhetorical. I didn't answer it. Janet and I had been through her hell together and she was now ready to live her life without regularly scheduled meetings with me.

At the door of my office she paused, turned around, and said, "I know you think it was psychoanalysis, Jim, but I think it was your love. But it doesn't matter." She left and I never saw her again.

Transference is an all-pervasive element in human life. It is active not only when we pick a mate but also as we choose our friends and enemies. It has an effect on where we shop, what TV programs we watch, what we read, and who we vote for. It will determine, for sure, whom we hire and maybe whom we fire. Because we are an ongoing compilation of experiences with others, transference affects all current and future experiences. It is a potent component of human nature. When we meet new people if we pause and listen, we will hear our unconscious mind immediately providing data about them. It's the easiest way to experience the unconscious mind at work.

11

Oh, No, Not Again!

Bad Broken Records

Albert Einstein, Benjamin Franklin and others supposedly said that insanity is doing the same thing over and over but expecting different results. If so, they were wrong. That is not insanity, but it is the hallmark of a psychological phenomenon called "the repetition compulsion."

To attain a grasp of the unconscious it helps to think of it as a tape player. If you don't change the tape it will continue to play the same songs over and over and over again. The repetition compulsion, which is in all human minds, is not always a bad thing, of course. Many people play happy, positive tapes. But whether an unconscious is upbeat and light or dark and destructive, be assured it will seek out the same people, and the same situations, resulting in the same psychodynamics, all through a person's life.

One of the clearest examples of the repetition compulsion can be found when a person has had multiple relationships, including marriages, that have turned sour. I had a patient named "Ginger" who grew up in a small town in South Dakota. Ginger married for the first time directly after high school. Her husband managed his grandfather's cattle ranch, was 6 feet 4 inches tall, with long blond hair and very muscular. Her second husband, whom she married at age twenty-six, was the owner of the town's drug store. He was 6 feet tall, crew cut, and obese. She married her third husband at age thirty-four. He was a diminutive man, about 5 feet 6 inches tall, and weighed no more than 140 pounds. He owned and operated a chain of auto body shops.

When Ginger came to see me, this third marriage was falling apart and she was in a heightened state of anxiety coupled with depression. Although she had little formal schooling beyond the twelfth grade, she was exceptionally bright and a dedicated reader. Ginger was certain that she was to blame for three failed marriages but had no idea what she was doing to cause the failures. "It must be all my fault," she cried during our first session. "All of my husbands are so different!" I asked her to describe them and when she did I had to agree Fabian, Fatty and Shorty did appear to be very different, but I knew they couldn't be.

And sure enough by the third session it became clear that the three men shared a number of similarities. All had a good sense of humor, they were dedicated to their jobs, none were close to their own families, none wanted children, none wanted Ginger to work outside the home. All three were borderline alcoholics and, occasionally, they all beat her up. Ginger kept picking abusive control freaks to be her loving wedded husbands. Bright as she was, she realized that when she dumped Shorty and went in search of husband number four, she would probably pick another guy who would beat her up. "Jim, you must help me. Why do I keep winding up with these pricks?"

I explained the repetition compulsion, told her it was coming from her unconscious, and that she should not blame herself. We then went to work piecing together her history before she ever met her husbands. It was not a pretty history.

Ginger's father, a heavy drinker, and her mother, a sometimes drinker, would occasionally have violent fights often ending with mom running to her bedroom and locking the door. The next day she'd be sporting a shiner along with bruised ribs. Ginger heard these fights, which occurred two or three times a year, as she cowered in her bedroom. After her mother left the fight scene, her dad would go to Ginger's room, take her clothes off and penetrate her. As he was doing this he told Ginger how much he loved her. Ginger's psychological history was disastrous.

During the periods of time between fights, the family appeared to be quite normal. Mom, who was not allowed to work outside of the house, prepared nutritious meals, kept a spotless home and made sure Ginger had the proper clothes to wear. She took an active interest in Ginger's school work and her friends. Dad, a master mechanic at the local Chevy dealership, made a good living and was always home after work. His relationship with Ginger during those normal times she described as "friendly." He liked to tease her but not in a cutting way. He could be very funny. On most Sundays the family attended church.

Over the many months of her therapy Ginger held on to the belief that "ninety-nine percent of the time I had a normal family life." She insisted that when pitted against the one percent terrible times it was not so bad overall. This was a defensive shield, a mask giving her the false belief that her childhood was nearly perfect. And she felt that the other families she had witnessed while growing up were much more unstable than hers. All my nudging, hinting and urging her to see that this was not so was to no avail. Ginger defiantly clung to the belief that her upbringing was mostly normal. I was ready to pull my hair out. Finally, out of desperation, I said to her, "Ginger, your father raped you two or three times a year for many years. This completely negates any of the nice things he did for you. And, Ginger, I'll bet you anything your mom knew what was going on."

That did it. The dam broke, and Ginger fell to pieces. When she began to compose herself, some twenty minutes later, she blubbered out, "I know she knew! She had to!" The sobbing began again.

One of the predominant characteristics of the unconscious mind is that it wants to repeat, over and over, the dynamics that make it up. One of the dynamics in Ginger's unconscious was that wives, from time to time, are supposed to be beaten by their husbands. She put that dynamic in place by choosing the three physically abusive guys she married. But she had another dynamic which added to her damaged psyche. After dad beat up mom, he went to Ginger for solace. Ginger was put in the role of "good wife," replacing mom. This dynamic consumed her with guilt and filled her with rage against her parents, which she deflected toward herself. She "won" the Oedipal conflict by replacing her mother, if only occasionally, and, therefore, deserved to be punished.

To begin the process of recovery, Ginger had to answer the question: "Why do I feel I must be punished by my husband?" To help her get started, I added, "When a person seeks punishment they must be feeling guilty about something. What, regarding your folks, do you feel guilty about?" It took us two years to answer that question, unscramble her feelings, and to turn her anger away from herself and to place it squarely where it belonged—directly at dear old mom and dad. By this time Shorty, who refused therapy, was long gone and Ginger was dating a guy who, at first, she was not attracted to but was now growing fond of. "Someday I might even love him," she laughed. Ginger was going to be okay.

Breaking one's repetition compulsions is never easy because they are so deeply ingrained in the unconscious mind. I used to tell my patients who were constantly finding themselves in lousy relationships, "If you are immediately attracted to someone, run like hell. That's your very powerful unconscious trying to set up its pre-programmed destructive dynamics." Though somewhat contrived, this advice was better than nothing until we could dig in.

My Own Undoings

One of the elements of my personal unconscious merry-go-round is the inclination to do good and then screw it up. This is known as "undoing" in psychoanalytic jargon and it teams up nicely with the repetition compulsion. I can trace this tendency back to grammar school. When in the seventh grade I was the "seventh man" on the basketball team. With four eighth graders graduating it was automatic, in my mind, that when I got to eighth grade I would be a starter. When eighth grade came and practice began, I acted cool, dogged it and looked down on other teammates. Before I knew what happened I was again the seventh man on the team picking up more splinters.

Once, in Little League, I hit a line drive like a rifle bullet that went between the center and right fielders. Knowing there was no way they could get to the ball in time to get me out (there was no outfield fence), I blithely started jogging around the bases. By the time I rounded third the fans and my teammates were screaming. I waved to them, mistaking their screams for cheers and continued to jog. I was thrown out at the plate.

I had an exceptional curve ball, and every time Butchie Johnson came up to bat all I had to do was throw him three curves and he'd strike out. Otherwise a very gifted athlete (you couldn't get a fastball by him), Butchie simply could not hit a curve. One time in the bottom of the seventh with two outs (in Little League we only played seven innings) Butchie came to the plate. Our team was ahead by one run and their team had one man on base. No problem. I had already struck Butchie out twice in the game so I threw two curve balls and he swung and missed both by a mile. To this day, some fifty years later, I can still recall what went through my mind. "I am going to show Butchie, my team, Butchie's team, and all the fans that I can strike out Butchie Johnson with a fast ball." I wound up and let it go and it was a good one—coming in low on the inside corner. Butchie swung and I think that ball is still going. He positively creamed it and we lost the game.

Remember, I was programmed "not to be another Bob, but to be a first Jim." I took this to heart. I had a Latin teacher in high school who had taught my scholarly brother eight years before me. Once he asked me to stay after school for a talk. He told me that I had the potential to be the best Latin student he ever taught and that included my brother. All I had to do was work a little harder. I was never so shocked in my life, did not believe him, and quit studying Latin. I wound up with a "C." (I still don't believe him.)

In college I tried out for the tennis team. Members were chosen through an elimination tournament. My high school, and others on the south side of Chicago, had no tennis teams. We only played intramural. I was the best player in my school but that really didn't count for much. In the college tryouts I found myself playing against a classmate, Dave McClenahan, who had been a member of his high school tennis team that won the Pennsylvania state championship. Dave and I began to play and I actually won the first few games, then this thought went through my mind, "I shouldn't be beating this guy. He was a state champ!" I promptly lost the first set and was demolished in the next. No college tennis for me. (Dave probably would have beaten me in any case but my self-diminishing pre-programming certainly made it easier for him.)

Also, while in college, I won the heart of a beautiful and wonderful girl. When Judy walked into a room all heads turned. We fell in love and dated regularly until I decided I should break up with her before she broke up with me. I knew that eventually she would learn what a boring, shallow guy I was.

And so it went into adulthood. In the Army, instead of playing it safe and staying on the ground as a Transportation Corps officer, running a motor pool, I volunteered to go to flight school. With this decision I wound up flying helicopters in the Vietnam War. Damn near got myself killed.

After the war, in my own business, I made a small fortune before I was twenty-eight years old and continued making big money selling condos in Florida. Then I moved to Colorado and you know that story. By the time my analytic training was over I was broke.

Of course, I had never put together this pattern of "do good then screw it up" until my analyst pointed it out to me and we spent many months dealing with it. Even to this day I've got to be on guard against it. Such is the power of the unconscious mind and its wish to repeat the same dynamics.

"Psychic determinism" is the cornerstone of psychoanalysis. It means that our emotions are built on previous emotional experiences. To demonstrate, here's one more story about Butchie Johnson. Before going to the first grade I prided myself on being the fastest runner of the ten or so little kids on our block. Early in the first grade our teacher, Sister Leonise, took us to Foster Park for an outing. We played games, had a picnic lunch and were generally enjoying ourselves when Sister said, "Come on, children, let's have a race!" I thought that was a great idea and as we got to the starting line I told Sister I was going to win, "Watch me, Sister!" I crowed for all to hear.

Our class consisted of kids from all over the parish, not just my block, and Butchie Johnson was one of them. Before that day I'd paid scant attention to him. Not only did Butchie beat me but so did another kid. I was devastated.

Sister Leonise, an angel in a habit, came over to me and put her cloaked arm around my shoulder. "You did really well, Jimmy. You came in third out of all those children." Her kind words didn't help as I realized, for the first time, there's a big world out there and there are a lot of Butchie Johnsons in it.

There is no doubt in my mind that if six years after the race some kid other than Butchie was standing at the plate I would have thrown that third curve ball. But I wanted revenge on Butchie by blowing a fastball by him. I wanted to embarrass him as he embarrassed me in first grade.

Years ago I had forgotten about the race but the memory was resurrected when I wrote about the curve ball incident. (I had never forgotten that.) No thought, feeling or memory exists alone. And if I ever encounter Butchie Johnson again I will not succumb to the repetition compulsion by trying to get the better of him. I've been psychoanalyzed. I'll buy him a drink.

12

Gotcha

The Pain in the Ass People

Rush hour traffic is heavy in all directions as you come to a red light. You are in the left lane with one car in front of you. The driver signals for a left turn, which is what you are going to do. When the light changes to green the car in front does not move forward into the intersection. The man doesn't budge until the light goes to yellow then slowly makes his turn. It is now red, leaving you sitting there forced to wait for the next change of lights. He "gotcha"—adding at least a minute and maybe more to your trip home. He also got you by raising your blood pressure and making you say bad words. You have just been the victim of "passive aggression."

Passive aggression is one of the negative personality traits that is rooted in the anal phase of emotional development. (The car's ass end was in your face.) Throughout the day we see and experience it frequently. Passive-aggressive personalities are everywhere and if they weren't so aggravating it would be fun to observe them, knowing that below their often pleasant, conscious persona lies anger, frustration and a need to control that irritates their family, friends, co-workers and strangers. Passive aggressive people are not persnickety about who they "get." Everyone's fair game.

The distinction between active aggressive behavior and passive aggressive behavior is obvious. Active aggression is overt, simple and straightforward, such as a punch in the nose or a slap to the face. Passive aggression is subtle, done unconsciously, and can take an infinite variety of forms. Defending against it is often impossible.

85

The Mind and I

People who regularly engage in acts of passive aggression are consciously unaware of what they are doing and, in some cases, think they are being extra nice. "Would you like chocolate, strawberry or vanilla ice cream with your birthday cake, Aunt Penelope?"

"Oh it doesn't matter, dear, whatever you have the most of, and if there's not enough cake I don't really need any." Nice, huh? Thoughtful, generous and self-sacrificing?

No. Penelope is now forcing you to make the decision for her, and you can bet she'll let you know it was the wrong one. "Oh my, chocolate ice cream on chocolate cake! That's different." Sweet little old Aunt Penelope got you. If only for a minute you were under her control.

Just as none of us can avoid passive aggressive people, we "normal" people will, from time to time, engage in it. For instance, my wife, Barbara, and I took a two-week trip to celebrate our twenty-fifth wedding anniversary, staying in hotels and sharing a bathroom. (We each have our own at home.) During the first few days I was driving her nuts by forgetting to put the toilet seat back down. At first she got angry but then decided to make a game of it. "Every time you leave the toilet seat up you owe me $5." I agreed. We had ten days left on the trip. I quickly did the math and calculated I could lose about $350. I am proud to report I only owed her $45 when we got home.

Passive aggression, like all personality faults, can be judged by degrees of severity. Recently I asked Barbara to rate my passive aggression on a scale of one to ten, ten being the worst. I was writing this chapter and felt it appropriate to 'fess up to whatever she said. (I figured it would be around a four.) She thought about it for a moment and said, "When we were first married I'd have called you a five. But after all these years I don't see it any more except for the toilet seat when we travel. So I'll call you a one. Which reminds me, you owe me $45. Are you ever going to pay up?" I really should pay her the money but I keep "forgetting" to get cash at the bank. (Forgetting is another form of passive aggression.)

Let's look at some more passive aggressive examples like, say, not paying your debts. I do not mean your mortgage payment, the electric bill, or the car payment. You will pay those, or else. I mean the debts from toilet seats left up, your lousy golf game, the Super Bowl wager, the twenty bucks you borrowed from a friend, the money you promised to chip in for Sally at the office who's having a baby, etc. Little things. Last year I had a friendly ten-dollar bet with a guy regarding the outcome of a football game. He lost but didn't pay me and he's a millionaire. I suppose he's waiting for me to "remind him" which is an additional way to control me, but I won't. I simply won't bet with him again. He got me.

Remembering that passive aggression is an anal trait, perhaps the classic passive aggressive act is using the last of the toilet paper and not getting a new roll for the next person. If he doesn't check to see there's toilet paper before doing his business you really got him good. As beads of sweat appear on his forehead, he frantically looks around for paper towel, tissue, newspaper, the wrapper from a bar of soap, the leaf of a house plant, anything! Eventually he'll open his wallet praying that there are one dollar bills in there. Perfect.

Time is a commodity we all have a finite amount of, so being late is another way to passively aggress. When people are waiting for someone there is nothing else they can do but wait. Five minutes, ten minutes, a half hour or more of a person's time can be consumed. The goal of a passive aggressive personality type is to subtly control other people.

Being too early also works well. Show up a half hour before a party is supposed to start as the host and hostess are scurrying around attending to last minute details. They'll be so happy to have their attention diverted by you. And be sure you insist on helping. That will even further distract them.

If you want to practice being passive aggressive, grocery stores are full of possibilities. Frequently leave your shopping cart to go hunt for an item, parking it in the middle of an aisle or up tight next to those items that most people need—the milk or hamburger sections are good. If there's a Take-a-Number dispenser at the deli leave your cart right in front of it. At the check-out counter be sure you question the clerk about the prices of certain items. Drag out a fist full of coupons and ask her to match them up. Be sure some are expired. Oversee the bag boy's loading of your purchases. Make him rearrange the cabbages and cans. Don't begin writing your check until you get the total and take time to balance your checkbook before moving on. The people behind you will wish for your death.

There are, obviously, hundreds of ways to passively aggress. (The only good thing about the behavior is that it beats the alternative—that punch in the nose.) Talking during movies or plays. Interrupting conversations. Mumbling. Asking a question then not listening to the answer. Leaving your incessantly barking dog outside—morning, noon and night. Walking it off the leash. Not cleaning up after it. Wearing perfume that overwhelms. Not bathing. If your kid cries in church or the movies, don't take him outside. Take your unruly children to expensive adult restaurants. Let them run around.

Talk loudly, and sound important, on your cell phone in public places. The invention of the cell phone has been one of the greatest boons in history for passive aggressives. With it they can make and receive calls to interrupt conversations, to disrupt meals and to ignore friends and family members. Their cell phones give them a newfound source of power, importance and means to control.

I was in a crowded area of the Tampa airport waiting to board a plane. Also there was a young corporate type who started making calls on his cell phone reminding people about a meeting. Rather than removing himself to a secluded area he remained smack in the middle of the crowd talking much louder than necessary and reminding his callers that "the dress is business casual." He repeated this over and over. Obviously the asshole just learned a new phrase. None of us could concentrate on our magazine articles, books or even our thoughts. With his cell phone and loud voice Mr. Business Casual was able to wipe out twenty minutes of many people's lives. We wanted to strangle him. We should have.

The Devil's Alive

The seeds for passive aggressive behavior are planted at about two years of age but to really get good at utilizing it you need to get into your teens. Teenagers are the undisputed masters of passive aggression. My psychoanalyst friend, Veryl, now retired, still consults with up-and-coming therapists. Veryl has a gift for getting to the core of an issue. Once we attended a seminar with members of the local analytic community and several religious leaders. We were asked to find the commonality, if any, among Jesus, Freud, Buddha and Jung, and the discussions were beginning to get heated. Veryl piped up and said, "Excuse me, but I think there is one thing we can all agree on: teenagers are the devil."

A teenager will drink all of the milk out of a bottle, put the cap back on, and return it to the refrigerator. They'll borrow a car and return it on empty, keeping the radio volume turned up to the max, so when you start the car you'll think a bomb went off. How big is your water heater? Just big enough for one teenager's shower. The rest of the family will have to wait until the water warms up again.

A man got me pretty good a few years ago. I walked into his store and this thirty-something owner, whom I had recently met, said, "Hi there, young man." He had attempted to be clever but he hurt my feelings. He made me feel like a man who looks old, so that calling me young was humorous. Forgiveness is good, as you'll recall, so after briefly deciding to boycott his business I chose instead to just chalk it up to his inexperience, youth and poor breeding.

I saw him a few weeks later at a meeting and he introduced me to a lady telling her I had written a "really interesting" book that was recently published. The lady was duly impressed, and I was pleased with myself for having forgiven the man's previous passive aggression. But then he told the lady my book was about my experiences in World War II. He was not trying to be funny, it was an honest mistake. (The book is about my experiences in Vietnam.) I went home and examined my face in the mirror, to be sure I still looked sixty and not eighty-five, and now I'll definitely be boycotting the bastard's store.

Not long ago a truly old guy got me. I was standing at the paint counter at Lowe's waiting for my paint cans to finish vibrating when I heard, "I don't have to paint anymore. I figure sixty-one years is enough years to work. I started working when I was eleven." I turned to see a man on my left talking to me.

"That's nice," I said and went back to staring at the jiggling cans.

"I think it was in 1957 or 1958," he continued, "'57 I'm pretty sure. I was building houses and I asked this young kid to hand me a level and he didn't even know what it was. Kids today don't know half of what we knew. But later I heard he became a carpenter. Ain't that a good one?"

"Yep," I replied still staring ahead. (Kids today. 1957?)

He continued, "The trim on my house is gray. Always has been and always will be. I don't like change. What color's the trim on your house?"

"White," eyes straight forward. (Don't let him suck me in.)

"That gets too dirty. You ought to make it gray."

Now I said nothing.

"Yep, it's silly to have white trim. You ought to change to gray."

I looked at him again and said, "I don't like change," figuring surely that would shut him up. Not a chance.

"What kind of paint do you like best?"

"What do you mean?" (He had me.)

"You know, the brand. I never buy paint here at Lowe's. Sears has the best. What kind of paint are you buying?"

Mercifully my paint was ready. I took the cans, looked at him and said, "I buy whatever my wife tells me to buy. She does the painting. I don't know how." And I walked off. (Got him back.)

There's two ways of looking at that encounter: (1) A lonely old man tried to engage a stranger in conversation and I was semi-rude, or (2) A passive aggressive old peckerhead saw an opportunity to verbally torture a stranger who was trapped in a place from which there was no escape, and I was semi-rude. I, of course, think it was mostly the latter.

Controlling by making noise is a great way to passively aggress. Hear the ear-splitting bangs and pops from the motorcyclist's *tail* pipe? He's vicariously using the bike to blow farts. Hear the ear-splitting noise from the young punk's car radio? For some moments you can't hear yourself think. But the noise itself is not totally anal. Part of it is oral. The boom, boom, boom in the background are farts but the melody is the baby crying for attention. It's a "two-fer."

Passive aggression is one of the most difficult personality disorders to treat because it comes from the anal phase of development, which is pre-verbal. People who are passive aggressive do not suffer from it because they have no idea what they are doing. Thus they never seek treatment for their malady.

Marriage counselors do see passive aggressives, however, because it is often one of the causes of marital meltdown. Living with a severe passive aggressive can be a nightmare. They leave their "shit" all over the house; they are always forgetting to do things promised; they are invariably late, and they pester—"Where's this? Where's that?" Cleaning up "behind" themselves would never cross their minds.

Other offenders are those who go on diets. I love to cook, but I have a son (you know who you are) who does not eat certain food groups. Cooking for him is not fun, it's irritating. How can someone eat a steak without baked potato? Ludicrous. What good is spaghetti without the pasta? Foolishness. Pork chops without rice and gravy? Ridiculous. Bacon and eggs without toast? Sacrilegious. If he cooked for himself that would be fine, but he can't boil water so he expects me, or his mom, to cook, all the while he's controlling the menu. Dieters have ingeniously found a way to passively aggress under the guise of being "good." Their dieting addictions are often unconsciously used to control others.

13

Dreams

The Royal Roads

At a social gathering I am introduced. The conversation goes like this:

MUTUAL FRIEND: "Helen, I'd like you to meet Jim Joyce."
HELEN: "Hi, Jim, its nice to meet you." (We shake hands.)
ME: "Nice to meet you, too, Helen."
MUTUAL FRIEND: "Helen is the owner of Gallery One, the furniture boutique on Loomis Boulevard at 79th Street.
ME: "I've been in your place. You have some really nice things."
HELEN: "Thank you, Jim, and what do you do?"
ME: "I'm a psychoanalyst. I have a private practice not far from you on Racine Avenue at 78th Street."
HELEN: "A psychoanalyst! Oh my, I'd better watch what I say," she laughs, "you might be psychoanalyzing me."
ME: "Don't worry about that," I laugh back, "psychoanalysis is hard work. I only do it when someone's paying me."

I, and every shrink I know, have had that conversation more times than we can count. And you know what? I've just told Helen a half-truth because we are psychoanalyzing as we stand together chatting. We don't have any choice. We don't listen like normal people. Nor do we think like them. We have this gift-curse which cannot be completely turned off. Now you know. If you don't want a shrink to know anything about you, you'd better walk away. Because as soon as you start talking you will be revealing things you've no idea you are revealing.

No, we won't be able to tell if you murdered someone in the past, or if you just made love in the guest room, or if you are divorced three times or six times, or if your father is on the FBI's Ten Most Wanted list.

92

But we can tell rather rapidly your dominant personality type—oral, anal, phallic—your degree of self-worth, your intelligence level, your "need to control" barometer, your histrionic level and numerous other generalities.

If the chat lasts for, say, twenty minutes we'll probably know how your marriage is doing, if you are a good parent and if you have unresolved issues with your own parents. To learn those things are we reading your mind? No. We'll know them because you'll tell us and you'll have no idea you are doing it.

Some people will take a social meeting with a psychoanalyst one step farther by telling him their dreams.

> HENRY: "Do you ever try to interpret people's dreams?"
>
> ME: "Sometimes, but they can be really confusing." (In reality they are very much a part of psychoanalysis and are the quickest way to learn about the patient's unconscious.)
>
> HENRY: "I had this really interesting dream the other night," or "I have the same dream over and over. Do you want to hear it?"
>
> ME: (Oh, God, No!) "Sure, as long as you don't expect me to know what it means." He didn't hear my disclaimer: he has already started in, and now you know why shrinks are reclusive. We can't go anywhere without getting nailed.

Dreams have been called "The Royal Road to the Unconscious" because they cut to the essence of people's psychic makeup by revealing their fears, guilts, conflicts, confusions, desires, and dreads. They also may reveal repressed artistic talent and spiritual longing. Dreams usually spring from the id or libido, chronicling their constant battle with the superego. They may, though rarely and not with everyone, also come from the ego. (Have I just put you to sleep?) Please, bear with me. To grasp the psychic dynamics of emotional life a conversational awareness of these terms is needed. They are frequently used in literature. Trust me, they're simple.

- Id = The source of psychic (emotional) activity. The id says, "Gimme, gimme, gimme, and get out of my way." When you think of the id, think of a kid—about 2½ years old.
- Libido = Sexual drives. Some analysts think it is part of the id. Others say it's separate. It doesn't matter.
- Superego = Your conscience—what's right and wrong for you.
- Ego—You. The person who has evolved into adulthood. The ego

mediates the struggle between your wants (id and libido) and your can't haves (the superego). Most of these push-pull interactions take place in the unconscious mind and they are constant even as we sleep.

The relationship among these entities is also easy to grasp. The id or libido says, "I want!" The superego then says, either "yes" or "no." If this interaction takes place in the conscious mind no problem. We've heard it. If the id or libido say "I want" in the unconscious mind and the answer is "yes," also no problem. We're on autopilot.

But when the id or libido says "I want" and the superego says "no," in the unconscious mind we do have a problem. We've reached a stalemate and something's got to give. Enter now the unconscious part of the ego that says, "I have an idea, let's compromise." And that compromise becomes a large part of our emotional state as our egos mediate between our sexual and aggressive primitive drives and our learned sense of right and wrong.

These psychic interplays of wants, can't haves and compromises can be upsetting because we are consciously unaware of them and they become causes of emotional distress. We don't realize what we are asking for. Now enter the ego, as mediator, using frustration, depressions, phobias, guilt, fears and anxiety as unholy replacements for the forbidden desires. It's a dirty trick playing out in our minds and we've no idea what the hell's going on.

For instance, 15 year old "Stephanie" overhears her mother say that she will never be as pretty as her older sister, Anna. "Stephanie doesn't have the bones," said mom.

Stephanie is stunned and crushed by Mom's appraisal and has the fleeting fantasy of pushing Anna (she's always been haughty) down a flight of stairs breaking some of those beautiful bones. She then immediately dismisses this cruel thought, relegating it to her unconscious. She is ashamed of herself and soon it is forgotten.

But it's only forgotten in her conscious mind. It will now live in her unconscious mind, dastardly though it is, perhaps for years. The ego now must compromise and does so by making Stephanie overly solicitous toward her sister. Over time she develops a newfound respect for Anna and a deeper love—consciously. Unconsciously she still wants to push the haughty bitch down the stairs. This ego compromise has a fancy name, *reaction formation*. It's a first cousin to *counterphobia*, which you'll meet in Chapter 16.

Another example: One day George notices that his son, "George, Jr.," standing out by the pool, has a newly developed manly physique. He immediately imagines his son having sex with his girlfriend, also at the pool, and on the heels of that he imagines himself having sex with the girl and soon both of them ... my God! Where is this going? What a sick thought! He banishes it.

Of course it isn't banished, it's just buried and what will George's ego do to keep it so? A compromise. From now on Big George will begin finding faults with Little George's girlfriends (none are good enough for him) to include the woman he eventually marries. Then an emotional barrier has been established between George and his son. It could last for the rest of their lives.

The purpose of ego compromises is to distance our conscious minds from the nasty parts of our unconscious ids. Oh so much better to admit to them, think them through and let them vanish on their own.

We analysts listen to our patients talk about their anxieties, etc. and we sort them out over time. This, alone, is effective, but another way to get to the core of conflicts, and much faster, is by listening to our patient's dreams. Thousands of books and articles have been written on the meaning of dreams. Dreams have been an integral part of literature, found in all cultures, going back to the beginning of recorded time. The Bible, for instance, is full of them. I have been listening to, and analyzing them, for thirty years and I am pretty good at it. Here's what I've learned.

We dream in symbols, which is the language of the unconscious, and symbols in dreams are unique to the dreamer. Therefore no one can tell what dreams "mean" without the candid participation of the dreamer. For instance, I had a patient, "Rita," who grew up on a ranch in Montana. One night she had a dream with a horse in it. Another patient, "Gene," grew up in the Bronx and he, too, dreamed about a horse. The horse in these two dreams is a symbol, and it is fair to assume that a horse will not have the same meaning in the unconscious minds of these two people from such different backgrounds. It is only by asking them what thoughts a horse brings to their minds that its symbolism will show itself.

Rita began talking about horses by saying how she loved them and spent untold hours riding them on the ranch. But then she remembered a time when a cowboy on the neighboring ranch got kicked in the head by a horse and has never been the same. He had been her boyfriend. "It's like he became a different person," she said. "He could go for hours without talking and then go into fits of rage. The horse kicking him in the head made him crazy."

I asked her if there was any way she could relate this memory to herself and she said, "Yes, I think I'm going crazy! That's why I'm here," and she began to sob.

Gene, from the Bronx, told me that when he was growing up he had seen a horse only once. His parents were divorced and he lived with is mother, his father having disappeared when Gene was seven years old. His mother told him his dad was a hopeless alcoholic. Gene said he didn't remember much about his father, didn't miss him, and rarely thought of him. The few things he did remember were pleasant—going with him to the combination tavern and pool hall, and playing catch with a baseball on the sidewalk in front of the house.

When I asked him to tell me as much as he could recall about seeing a horse as a kid he said there were actually six or eight of them. "My mother took me to a parade and there were these huge horses, I know now they were Clydesdales, pulling a wagon. I couldn't believe how big they were and I got real close to them."

"What kind of wagon were they pulling?" I asked.

"It was a Budweiser wagon loaded with cases of beer," he said.

"What comes to mind about Budweiser?"

"That's what my dad drank. I used to get him cans from the refrigerator."

"And you're sure you don't miss him?"

"Maybe I do," he said, eyes now brimming with tears.

Gene and Rita both had dreams with a horse in them but that symbol had different meanings. To Gene it was the painful longing for his dad. To Rita it was her fear of losing her mind. Over the years they must have had many dreams expressing those emotions. Gene admitted he had always missed his dad but would never say so because that would hurt his mother. Rita had felt there was something wrong with her mind from as early as age twelve, years before her boyfriend's tragedy. But neither could recall ever dreaming about a horse. Gene had dreams with other symbols that could take him to the same place, however: billiard balls, baseball gloves, a refrigerator and, once, a friend whose nickname was Bud. All of these symbols were not that far removed from his dad in the mysterious ways of the unconscious.

Most dreams are not as clear and easy to figure out as these two, but there would have been no way for me to analyze them without the patient's input. Our dreams are our creations and, therefore, are unique to us and all symbols in them have personal meanings, no matter how insignificant they may appear.

Why can't dreams be straightforward? Why couldn't Rita have dreamt about her cowboy boyfriend and have him segue into her? Why couldn't Gene have dreamt about his dad, as he remembered him, beckoning to him? Why all this symbolic confusion? The theory is that the real meanings of these kinds of dreams are too painful, fearful or guilt-producing for the conscious mind to deal with. So we "repress" them into the unconscious where they lurk in symbolically disguised form. I believe this theory is correct regarding most of our dreams.

The meanings of dream symbols are discovered by conscious "associations" to them. Symbols in our minds hang around together, like those birds of a feather that flock together. If someone dreams about a horse, or a flight of stairs, or flying, or falling, or being chased, or butterflies or any one of a zillion things and wants to know their meanings, he should start talking freely, without conscious editing. He should say, out loud, whatever pops into his mind no matter how silly, embarrassing, or seemingly far afield. This is called "freely associating" and, with the help of a trained analyst, patterns will begin to emerge. With enough time, candidness, and diligence the dream symbols will reveal their meanings. When they do a person will know, without doubt, when truth has been discovered. It's an amazing and thrilling—"Wow! That's it!"— kind of experience very similar to an insight. Seemingly unscientific, to be sure, but the end result is undeniable. The person just learned something major about himself.

When we return to a physical place from our past like a town we'd lived in, a school we'd attended, or to an old neighborhood, upon getting there we will begin to experience memory after memory "associated" with that place. Had we not gone there those memories would not have been recalled—brought into consciousness. This is analogous to dream symbols. Hiding in the dark behind the symbol will be memories and feelings from the past, but we won't get to them unless we "go" there.

Because dreams speak from the unconscious mind it is best not to ignore them. Psychoanalytic thought is: to remember dreams is good; to tell them to someone is better; to have them analyzed is best.

Why not leave well enough alone and blow off remembering dreams and talking about them? If someone is a happy, upbeat, contented, non-frustrated, "life couldn't be better" person—I agree, blow them off. He's got his emotional life knocked. On the other hand, even the most wonderful among us could be better. No one is without dark, secretive, painful parts of himself lurking in his unconscious mind. No one.

Some people say, "I don't dream," or "I don't remember my dreams," but unless they're brain dead they do dream. If a person consciously tells himself to remember his dreams, just before he goes to sleep, he'll begin to.

One Tough Case

In all the years I practiced, only once did I feel it necessary to ask a medical doctor colleague to prescribe an antidepressant, Elavil, for a patient. "Jo Anne" was in her late twenties, attractive, intelligent, college educated and seriously depressed. She was a referral from her OB-GYN, whom she'd been seeing in an attempt to get pregnant. She'd been married to "Tom" for five years. The first four years they practiced birth control and now wanted to start a family. There seemed to be no physical impediments to pregnancy. Her depression began shortly after she got off the pill and had become progressively worse. It was now overwhelming her. She couldn't talk without crying and admitted to suicidal thoughts. Her doctor was concerned and after our first session so was I. The Elavil did the trick, however, and after a week or so it kicked in and she perked up, felt a little better, and our therapy began.

13. Dreams: The Royal Roads

Jo Anne's history was unimpressive, analytically speaking. She had a younger brother with whom she got along "great." Her parents were described as "loving" to their children and to each other. She could recall no childhood trauma. Her earliest memories were playing with dolls, with her mom, in her bedroom. Perfect. After four or five sessions I was stymied. We made no progress, we had no revelations. Were it not for the drug I believe Jo Anne would have reverted to her very deep funk. She and I were floundering. Her past and present circumstances gave me no clue as to why she'd become so depressed.

Then we got lucky. Jo Anne came to the next session, sat down and said, "I finally remembered a dream. I haven't dreamed in years. Do you want to hear it?" I had asked about her dreams in every previous session. I practically shouted, "Yes!"

Note: Psychoanalysts break a dream down into three distinct parts: (1) *The manifest dream*—what is remembered upon waking (2) *The dream work*—the ego using symbols to disguise the dream's message (3) *The latent dream content*—what the dream is really telling us.)

"It is very short. Is that okay?"

"That's fine," I said and wanted to kiss her. At last her unconscious would give us a peek.

"I was on an airplane flying to England. I was supposed to meet the Queen Mother but when I got there she changed her mind and refused to see me. I didn't care. That's all I can remember."

Now we had some symbols. A trip, flying, the vessel airplane, a foreign country, rejection, denial, a queen, and a mother. All we had to do was figure out what they were hiding to find a clue to Jo Anne's depression.

The complete theory of dreams is somewhat tedious, but a key element is: we dream in "primary process," meaning each symbol is a condensation of numerous thoughts, feelings, and, perhaps, memories. Primary process is like the ten-month-old learning to talk. He says "goo-goo." This means to him: I am hungry and thirsty. Get me juice, macaroni and cheese, applesauce. Put me in my high chair. Give me my spoon. Turn on Sesame Street. Be quick about it.

Or he'll say "gah-gah." This means put on my jumpsuit and hat. Put me in the stroller and take me for a walk. Stop at the store for ice cream and at the funny dog's house who wags his tail. Be quick about it. (Mothers know the difference between goo-goo and gah-gah.)

Jo Anne's dream led us to the following memory and revelation. When I asked her what came to mind about traveling to a foreign country she said a year earlier she and three girl friends had taken a road trip to Canada. None had been out of the United States and thought it would be neat to go across the border. Tom and the other husbands agreed and off the women went.

The interstate highway system would have gotten them to Canada in two days so they decided to take the lesser highways through rural America. Each night they stayed in little motels in out-of-the way towns and plotted the next day's journey. They'd take five days to go up and two days back. And that's when Jo Anne remembered.

"I couldn't believe it. I wasn't paying any attention to the route we were taking. It was just fun being with my friends. 'Diane' was driving and she stopped for lunch at a little café in this tiny town in Minnesota. We went inside and sat by the window. I looked across the street and saw the bank building. My heart started pounding and I wanted to scream. It was horrible!" She started to cry.

I was, of course, baffled. When she composed herself I said, "Jo Anne, you've lost me. What about the bank building?"

"That's where it happened!"

"What happened?"

"In that doctor's office above it. That's where I had my abortion!"

"Jesus Christ, what abortion?" I unprofessionally blurted.

"When I was eighteen!" she yelled and the tears became rivers.

And now we knew. (I'll tell you the rest of the story but back to the dream symbols for a moment.) The trip is obvious. England is a foreign country closely tied to Canada. The penis airplane made her pregnant, but because she rejected the baby, Queen "Motherhood" rejected her. But she didn't care, denying her feelings.

Jo Anne had wanted to marry "Eddie," the boyfriend who got her pregnant. Not only would he not marry her but he dumped her, although he did give her money for, and insisted upon, the abortion. It took us months to work through this horrible time in her life. She was amazed at the depth of her guilt about the abortion, saying that at the time it was simply the thing to do. "Everybody got abortions. What was the big deal? They were legal and everything. I thought nothing of it. I was just crushed by being dumped by my boyfriend."

The abortion had affected her more than she had been willing to admit, and our sessions dealt primarily with that guilt. Her ambivalent feelings were also discussed and the number of ramifications of that decision of so long ago. She now became aware that over the years she'd had fleeting thoughts that were immediately dismissed: How old would the baby be now? Was it a boy or a girl? What would I have named it? Would Eddie love it? Would I still be married to Tom?

Soon Jo Anne was now talking freely, her mood much improved. I explained during one session that guilt can adversely affect bodily functions and suggested that maybe that's why she was not able to conceive. Her jaw dropped. Then she said, "You know what? In the far back of my mind I hear this little voice say, 'You don't deserve a baby!' My God could it be that simple?" In time and with lots and lots of talk, Jo Anne's depression went away. A year after we terminated she had her baby. Thank you, Elavil, for the kick start. Thank you, dreams, for the clue. God save the Queen.

Strangely, abortions are not always guilt producers. Some women, along with their men, can have them and seem to go on with their lives never looking back. This was not the case with Jo Anne. As she relived the experience in therapy she had three distinct memories of her thought process during that time. "(1) I must abort this child, because Eddie insists. (2) But if I get rid of the baby, Eddie will take me back. (3) Then we'll get married and have another baby to make up for it."

This conflict between the id (get rid of the baby) versus the superego (it's the wrong thing to do), accompanied by the ego's rationalization (have another baby later), quickly found its way into Jo Anne's unconscious mind. At the time she was far more devastated by losing Eddie than by the abortion. He did not take her back, however, and eventually she got over him and continued with her eighteen-year-old life. But a time bomb was set and began to tick, exploding nine years later in the form of severe depression—the result of an ego compromise.

I had a marriage counseling case with a colleague. I saw the husband, a wealthy industrialist in his mid-fifties. She saw the wife, also in her mid-fifties. The husband had recently decided his wife must stop smoking because he had a nightmare (he woke up screaming) that she would soon die from the smoke. Her smoking had not bothered him before, but now he was preoccupied by it. They'd been happily married for four years. Because of his fear she underwent a complete physical examination and was declared exceptionally healthy. But that didn't allay the husband's anxiety. His obsession with her smoking was driving him crazy and wrecking the marriage. For her part she loved her husband, but she also loved to smoke and had been doing so for thirty years. She would not, could not, quit.

At first I did not like the man. He was a control freak who apparently always got his way. His wife had insisted on the therapy. He was not a happy participant. "This is a waste of time," he said. But by the third session he mellowed toward the process, telling me to ask him anything. "I want to get my money's worth." I was now able to maneuver him into his childhood and asked about his earliest memory. His eyes welled up. "The fire," he said.

"What fire?" I asked. He told me that when he was a little boy his family's home burned to the ground.

"That's the first thing I remember. The smoke rising from the rubble of our burned down house."

"How old were you?" I asked.

"Four," he said, "Everything was lost."

Our sessions took a wonderful turn toward positive as he got the connection I pointed out between his wife's smoking and his smoking first home; also the "four" connection between his age and their years of marriage. (The unconscious keeps a calendar of past events.) I could now forgive him his controlling ways. If my house burned down when I was four I'd have an inordinate need to control, too. And smoke was extremely frightening to his unconscious mind, which is why he dreamed about it in the form of a nightmare.

Our sessions ended shortly thereafter and the marriage continued happily onward. A specific problem was presented. We got to the core of it and it was resolved. Rarely, however, was it that simple.

Nightmares are usually easier to analyze than regular dreams because the messages are closer to the surface. They have burbled up to the almost pre-conscious level and when they break through, the ego doesn't have time to thoroughly edit (disguise) them. So we wake up in panic. Often nightmares echo, or mirror, past psychodynamics that are analogous to current ones. In the industrialist's unconscious mind, for instance, smoke symbolized a huge loss and he was terrified it would happen again, four years into his new life.

In my experience almost all dreams have to do with the repression of painful or unpalatable material. They vent sexual desires, aggressive impulses, deep hurts from the past and other events too embarrassing or painful for people to discuss, think about or admit to. We give Sigmund Freud (1856–1939) credit for discovering this. But there are other dreams that have a totally different "feel" to them. They have a spiritual quality and are free of angst and conflict. They seem futuristic and often prophetic. I refer to these as Jungian dreams, in deference to Dr. Carl Jung (1875–1961), who spent much of his career with the spiritual contents of the unconscious mind. These dreams also have repression as their cornerstone, but they are symbolizing repressed artistic talents and needs, inventions, original ideas, spiritual longings, life quests and even songs. Jungian dreams come from our higher nature which Freud paid little attention to. We don't hear them often.

I've had patients tell me dreams that had beautiful paintings, sculptures, poems, and stories in them. They were frequently in color and had a delightful flavor to them. The wise therapist jumps on these dreams and encourages the patient to take up chisel, brush, or pen. An artistic pursuit is one of the things people can do for their emotional well-being. It is a wonderful thing for patients and therapists to see the immediate improvement when the patients get into their creative side. Anxiety drops and depression lifts, as paintings come to be or poems emerge. The goal of analysis is to enhance people's abilities to love, work and *create*.

Be Careful

But a word of caution. If the analysis only accomplishes the unleashing of repressed creative needs and talents, then the analysis has failed. Being creative is important for emotional health but there's much more repressed than creativity. Mostly we repress the id and libido stuff—the nasty, embarrassing stuff—the stuff we all share on the primitive plane. If this isn't dealt with, and the therapy concentrates only on the spiritual and creative side of the patient, all the analyst has done is bring into being a creative neurotic. This is not a goal of therapy.

I had a dream that I was sure was Jungian in that it seemed to be prophetic, having nothing to do with repressed id and libido material. Barbara's only sibling, Cheryl, and her husband, Jim, lived on their sailboat at Phuket, Thailand. Although I have known them for twenty-seven years they'd never shown up as symbols in my dreams. On the night of December 26, 2004, I dreamed that Jim and Cheryl were lost at sea.

When we turned on the TV in the morning we saw, to our horror, that a gigantic tidal wave, a "tsunami," had hit Phuket. Hundreds of people were already reported dead and thousands were missing.

Barbara's mom was visiting us for the holidays and as the awful day progressed, with reports of death and devastation increasing, they agonized over the possibility, probability, that Jim and Cheryl were dead. I, of course, knew they were. The chances were terribly slim that I would dream about them, after twenty-seven years of not doing so, on the same night a rare tsunami hit their location. There was no doubt in my mind they were lost. What else could they be symbolizing in my unconscious? But I kept my mouth shut just in case.

For twelve hours we watched in agony as the news got worse and worse. We were well aware they often anchored their boat just a few hundred yards off shore. From the television coverage we knew they could not possibly have survived. (Eventually the count reached 200,000 killed throughout Asia.)

About 9 p.m. our phone rang. "Hi, it's Cheryl! We're fine! We were inland when the tsunami hit!"

So dreams that seem to be, without doubt, Jungian and prophetic may not be. The only other possible meaning to this dream, then, was that it came from my id. I then remembered, upon waking, having the fleeting thought that if Cheryl was dead Barbara would be the sole heir, meaning twice as much money for us. So it was, after all, a wish fulfilling, greedy dream of the Freudian type, reinforcing, once more, that we human beings are self-centered two-year-olds in our ids.

13. Dreams: The Royal Roads

Jungian psychology is the discipline of choice for many in the intellectual and academic community. Jung's emphasis was on our higher nature encompassing creativity and spirituality, and his research and findings were wonderful additions to the body of knowledge. But we must also deal with our basic needs and desires which are most unpleasant and are at the core of emotional illness. To run to the spiritual and stay there, ignoring the rest, would be a serious psychotherapeutic mistake.

Carl Jung, by the way, used Freud's astounding discoveries to create his own niche in psychology, taking many of Freud's basic concepts, embellishing them and putting his own names on them. He called Freud's unconscious "the shadow," for instance, certainly a cooler, hipper more mysterious name. It walked, talked and quacked like Freud's duck, however, but no big deal. Creative thinkers in both the arts and the sciences have been ripping each ... excuse me, borrowing from each other for centuries. Besides, jargon is mostly food for academics. In the room with the couch, feelings reign.

14

Herr Professor Doktor Sigmund Freud

Giant

Sigmund Freud, M.D., of Vienna, Austria, is known as the Father of Psychoanalysis. Note, that is the *Father*, not the founder. The founder was another medical doctor, Joseph Breuer, who was a friend and mentor to Sigmund. Dr. Breuer had a woman patient, the famous "Anna O.," who completely baffled him. She had multiple complaints including headaches, stomach aches, leg pains, chest pains, neck pains, dizziness, temporary loss of sight, temporary loss of hearing, temporary paralysis—you name it. She was a mess and none of Breuer's medicines were helping her.

So one day, out of frustration, Dr. Breuer asked his patient to talk about her life leaving out all of the physical ailments. The lady was verbose and freely discussed her current life and segued into her past life, telling him of unfortunate events in her childhood; over time, simply by talking, her symptoms disappeared. Breuer was at once intrigued and unnerved. It was contrary to his training and experiences that she could get better simply by talking about the bad things that happened to her in her youth. No way was he going to write this up for the medical journals; his peers would think he'd lost his faculties.

But he did confide his discovery to the young Dr. Freud, who was becoming disenchanted with traditional medicine. Breuer referred this patient to Freud, as well as other patients with apparent histrionic symptoms. Freud was grateful; he needed the business, and that's how "The Talking Cure" came to be.

While interviewing his patients Freud heard patterns emerge, many concerning sexual trauma in their early years. He deduced that trauma from years ago was having adverse, sometimes devastating effects on the patients' adult lives, manifesting in neuroses and innumerable physical complaints. Freud, a scientist, was as baffled as Breuer, but there was so much evidence to support his findings he could not ignore them.

He discovered there was a vast storehouse of feelings and memories which his patients had blocked from their consciousness, and he called this storehouse the "unconscious." This word had been used before but its meaning was nebulous (like subconscious is today.) Freud gave it structure and stature. Interestingly, it was his patient, Anna O, who suggested Freud change the name of his treatment from "The Talking Cure" to "psychoanalysis." She thought "Talking Cure" sounded unprofessional. Freud agreed.

Freud became especially interested in his patients' dreams, intuiting that they contained hidden messages that could be put to therapeutic use. He's the one who first called dreams "The Royal Road to the Unconscious," and he put together a theory on what dreams really mean. In 1900 he published his best known work, *The Interpretation of Dreams*, and the world hasn't been the same since.

He's Crazy

Early in his career as a psychoanalyst Freud gave a presentation of his findings to the prestigious Viennese Medical Society. Freud told these titans of medicine, in the most medically sophisticated city in the world, that he had discovered that not only could children's adverse sexual experiences cause problems later in their lives, but that children have sexual desires of their own. If Freud had told the good doctors he had recently contracted a case of crabs and was now spreading them around the room, he could not have become less popular. "Children have sexual desires? He's a pervert! He's out of his mind!" they said. From that day forward Freud was shunned by his medical colleagues in Vienna.

So with no help from his medical peers Freud discovered the stages of psycho-sexual (emotional) development, the repetition compulsion, and the phenomenon of transference. He developed the theory of the id, ego, and superego and how they interact, and revealed the intricacies of the Oedipal conflict. Along the way he picked up followers: Ernst Jones from England, Karl Abraham from Germany, Sandor Ferenczi from Italy and scores of others who knew he was onto something new and profound. Among these followers was Dr. Carl Jung of Switzerland.

Jung was enchanted by Freud for many years and the two became great friends, but eventually they grew apart. Jung came to believe there was much more to the unconscious mind than repressed sexual and aggressive impulses and expressed his beliefs to Freud. Freud thought this was too shallow and intellectual. It pissed him off and he told Jung so. The final split between Jung and Freud came over one of Jung's dreams, called "The cellar dream." Freud said it had to do with Jung's father. Jung said it had to do with repressed creativity. They disagreed so vehemently that a rift occurred that lasted for the rest of their lives. Any analyst listening to the dream today would say they could both be right because dreams, we've learned, are multi-dimensional, but neither man was good at compromise. It would be hard to find two bigger egotists than Carl Jung and Sigmund Freud.

You'd be surprised how many people hate Sigmund Freud. There are those, even with college educations, who consider Freud to be evil or, at best, a charlatan. The fact that you cannot see a movie, watch a play or read a book without experiencing his influence doesn't seem to register with them. And the fact that millions of people have been made whole by psychoanalysis goes right over their heads. I suppose they think it's a coincidence. Before Freud and the "Talking Cure," people with mental problems were left to flounder or were simply locked up.

Surprisingly, many of today's university professors of psychology, theology and philosophy also think Freud was a devil. Some actually blame him for today's sexual permissiveness, as though the man invented human nature, rather than merely explaining a part of it. Even more surprising than the academics discrediting Freud are the practicing psychologists, social workers, and other psychotherapists who go out of their way to denigrate him. If there was ever proof needed that we all harbor anger at our parents here is an example. Freud is the "father" of their career discipline, that is, letting people talk to get better—the healing treatment called psychoanalysis, which spawned all legitimate psychotherapies. Yet they denigrate him. Go figure. Before this book ends we'll discuss the type of folks who become shrinks. That will shed some light.

Freud worked in Vienna all his adult life. He loved the city and wished to retire and die there, but along came the Nazis who would have granted only one of those wishes. In 1938 when he was eighty-two years old he was forced to flee to England to save his life. Many of his relatives, including siblings, died in the camps.

Freud was the father of six children. When they were little and he was uncovering the mysteries of the unconscious mind, his wife, Martha, told him, "Don't you be experimenting with your new theories on the kids." He respected her wishes until his youngest daughter, Anna, came along. She worshiped her father and followed in his footsteps and became quite the psychoanalyst in her own right. Freud, himself, psychoanalyzed his daughter to prepare her for her career. (Generally considered to be a terrible idea.) At any rate Anna became a gifted child therapist but, of course, had no life of her own. She never married or had children. How could she? She was married to her father. In 1939, Anna killed her father by overdosing him with morphine when the pain from his jaw cancer became unbearable. She did so at his request.

One of my favorite stories about Freud was his counsel to those psychoanalytic students and colleagues whom he had trained. When it became clear that they had better get the hell out of Austria (they were almost all Jews), he encouraged the brighter ones to go to either England or South America. Those he secretly considered to be not quite up to par he encouraged to go to the United States. He figured they couldn't do any damage here because the people of the United States "wouldn't get it anyway." Freud didn't like the United States. He considered us too materialistic and cultureless.

And sure enough the psychoanalysts who arrived in New York City from Europe began training American analysts who soon began making up numerous petty, dumb rules on how to practice the discipline. It began to lose its soul. Freud became most upset, for instance, when the United States psychoanalysts decided that only medical doctors would become certified psychoanalysts. In 1926 he felt compelled to write a paper entitled "The Question of Lay Analysis" to set them straight. In it he stressed that psychoanalysis should not be restricted to the medical profession. They ignored him and his paper.

Our Determined Minds

The Interpretation of Dreams and numerous other works by Freud changed forever how people looked at each other and how they looked at themselves. The centuries old concepts of "the bad seed," when a person was deemed incorrigible or corrupt, and a deity making people happy or sad could now go the way of other erroneous concepts. With his discovery of *psychic determinism* Freud clearly demonstrated how a person's current emotional responses are influenced by previous emotional experiences and how a human being's emotional make-up is the result of an ongoing process beginning in earliest childhood.

Jung, too, was correct when he showed that dammed up creative juices can indeed cause frustration and anxiety. And there have been numerous others who've stood on Freud's shoulders and learned more about the intricacies of the unconscious mind.

Freud is hated by a variety of people for a variety of reasons. With his discovery of the power of the unconscious he seemed to relegate the concept of free will to the back burner, where it plays a barely active role in how we make decisions. Therefore many decisions that we believe are acts of free will are, simply, not. Freudian purists will tell you that all big decisions, like whom we decide to marry and what careers we pursue, as well as the little decisions, like ordering either chocolate or vanilla, are actually no decisions at all. They believe we are pre-programmed to make all decisions by our unconscious. I do not agree with them. I believe we can indeed exercise free will regarding the ice cream. But when it comes to whom we choose to marry, well, that's probably the most unconscious decision we'll ever make. There are too many factors buried deep in our minds that have been at play for too many years to allow us to meet a person, get to "know" him or her, and rationally (consciously) decide, "That's the one for me."

Ice cream, however, is easy. We can change favorites from vanilla to chocolate to rocky road as we go through life. But the type of person we are romantically attracted to will not change. The person of the opposite sex who rings our bell will have certain psychic dynamics that mesh with our own dynamics, or the attraction won't be there. This does not have to do with physical looks. Appearances can be vastly different in people who attract us. It must be a personality type putting out certain emotional vibrations that our unconscious picks up before we stand at the altar to say "I do."

Remember the Oedipal conflict: kid wants to "marry" the parent of the opposite sex, which takes place around age five and again at puberty. The kid's desires are denied, but they don't go away. When people enter their twenties and need arises to find someone, settle down, and start a family, who will they be attracted to? They'll be attracted to that first lost love or, more accurately, someone who reminds them of her or him. (Remember transference.) No experience goes away but it can be forgotten, as it sinks into the unconscious. People are going to marry their mother/father or some other early parental figure known as a "love object."

In the jargon of the profession, marriage is called "The Final Resolution of the Oedipal Conflict." Of course we do not consciously think of our spouse as a parental replacement but unconsciously he or she is, thus satisfying the repressed unconscious desires of years ago. That's one big conflict from the past which is now resolved and we can live happily ever after in marital harmony. Right? Right!

But ... only if! Only if the relationship with the parent of the opposite sex was a harmonious one. If it wasn't and, or, the spouse's wasn't, then we're in for a different kind of rocky road. We will unconsciously transfer feelings of anger onto our spouse that should have been vented at that flawed love object from our past—who our spouse represents. But how can a little kid yell at his parent? There always seems to be a catch.

Because this is not a book on marriage counseling we're going to continue to another topic. But trust me when I tell you that Oedi-pal problems are not only the major cause of divorce, they also cause more neuroses than any other factor. Freud figured this out early in his studies and announced it to the world. Many people resent him for that.

Kiss Your Kids. Doctor's Orders

Another good reason to resent Freud is because he laid so much responsibility on parents for how their kids turned out emotionally. Before he discovered that the family environment in which a child is raised can be a prime cause of depression, anxiety, and phobias, parents simply shrugged their shoulders when their adult children were screwed up. "We did the best we could," they'd say or, "Don't know what happened to Billy. We raised him up the same as all the others and they're fine." Freud showed that this attitude is no longer viable. The evidence is solid that parents are greatly responsible for their offspring's emotional lives. Go to any prison and get a family history from a sampling of prisoners. They did not grow up in a kind and gentle environment being loved without strings and being hugged and kissed regularly.

And parents do not treat all their children "the same." They may all have received the same allowance, good quality food, shelter, and clothing, and they may have attended the same schools. But are parents as concerned (panicked) when the third child wakes up in the middle of the night with a fever as they were with the first? Did they take as many baby pictures of number two as of number one? Did their hearts stop when number one cut his lip on the edge of the coffee table? Or when number four did it? And did they treat their sons exactly as they treated their daughters? Did they feel the same about them? Of course not.

Occasionally in my practice I saw siblings. Once it was two brothers and their sister. After hearing each of them describe their parents, there was no way I would have known they were talking about the same peo-ple, had I not known ahead of time. Whenever I saw siblings it was the same thing. Brothers and sisters telling me all about their parents, yet their descriptions of their folks' personalities, and how their parents treated them, were vastly different. It was amazing.

A Book

In 1946, *Baby and Child Care* by Benjamin Spock, M.D. was published, and the raising of children would never be the same. Prior to Spock's book all of the "experts" stressed rigidity and consistency in the raising of children, especially feeding times, sleeping times and potty training. Many of the experts strongly discouraged hugging and kissing children or even holding children on laps.

Doctor Spock was a pediatrician and a psychoanalyst. He served in the Army as a psychiatrist during World War II and it was during this time he wrote most of the book. Before the war Spock went through psychoanalysis in New York. It was that experience which spawned his child raising theories, some of which are:

- Parents know more than they think they do. They should trust their intuition.
- Children are individuals and should set their own schedules for eating and sleeping.
- Even if babies are not hungry but want breast or bottle let them have it. "Babies love to suck," said Spock, "It's good for them."
- Toilet training should never be forced. The kid will come around in his or her good time. "To force it," said Spock, "creates a No! adult."
- Use encouragement as much as possible, rather than discipline. (But he was not against discipline.)

Baby and Child Care was the largest selling non-fiction book (next to the Bible) in the twentieth century. Fifty-one million copies were sold and it was printed in 40 languages. It, more than any other single vehicle, spread Freud's discovery that experiences in childhood have a direct relationship to adulthood, but he was not credited. Doctor Spock told anyone who'd listen to him that his kindly, individualistic child raising ideas were a *direct* result of his personal psychoanalysis and training but, in his books he did not mention Freud by name or use his jargon. He was writing for "folks."

Nowadays, thanks to Freud, people can no longer simply "have" children. Now they must pay attention to their developing psyches, as well as provide food, clothing and shelter. The old expression "Children should be seen and not heard" has gone the way of the steam engine and we can thank Sigmund for that.

An Unhealthy Commandment

One of the Ten Commandments is to *Honor thy father and thy mother*. Honor means respect, so for thousands of years Jews, then Christians, then Muslims have been commanded by their God to do something that may not always be appropriate. This can be a real eye-crosser, one of the greatest mixed messages of all time. God commands someone to respect her mother who's passed out drunk on the couch and her father who left her without so much as a good-bye when she was ten? That's asking the impossible of the unconscious mind.

Honor (respect) is the word that has come down through time, yet it's psychologically unhealthy to attempt to respect people who have consistently treated you with disdain. People say they respect these kinds of parents, and fervently believe it on the conscious level, but their unconscious knows better. They are giving themselves a mind-torque which can make them emotionally ill.

The conscious and unconscious minds should be in sync as much as possible. That's a goal of psychotherapy. The unconscious knows the truth, because it was an eyewitness, but the conscious mind is always trying to make nice by cleaning up the past, and by doing so causing inner turmoil. Freud discovered this.

I am not against the Ten Commandments or religion in general. I am a believer. But it is clear that we humans sometimes put words into God's mouth (which is what I am about to do). Instead of it being "Honor thy father and thy mother," what God surely meant was "Understand thy father and thy mother" and then, if necessary, forgive them. That makes a lot more sense, emotionally speaking.

According to the Gospel of John, 8:32, Jesus said, "The truth shall set you free." I think it's neat that this could also be the slogan of psychoanalysis. When the truths from our pasts are relived, felt and acknowledged, no matter how painful this might be, we are going to get better. Freud learned this truth about truth and passed it along. Yet this is unpalatable for many people. One has to wonder what their objection is to personal enlightenment. They've got to be afraid of something, but what? Insight, growth, emotional boat rocking? It's befuddling, but I suspect it's resentment. Our emotional lives are mostly the making of others, which is a bitter pill to swallow for those who secretly resent those makers. They want to distance themselves from them proclaiming "I am my own person!" But the process of analysis takes them back to their emotional beginnings, which clearly demonstrate, "No you're not!" (Damn you, Freud.)

Freud's observations and insights took some of the nonsense out of life and they permeate and have advanced Western civilization. And they will not go away because, as Plato said, "Once lit the flame of truth will not go out." And Carl Jung, too, advanced civilization with his insights into our higher nature. But you want to hear something ironic? In their personal lives Carl Jung (Dr. Spiritual), the son of a Christian minister, was embarrassingly promiscuous. On the other hand, Sigmund Freud (Dr. Sex), an atheist and lapsed Jew, was essentially a prude. People are something else. Let's talk about eagles.

15

Use Eagles, If Necessary

Breaking Protocol

Early in our training we were taught that our most important tool was our intuition, the heart and gut being more attuned to emotions than the logic of the brain. Intuition, we learned, superceded academic knowledge and could also overrule guidelines on how to conduct psychoanalytic sessions. My time with "Erica" demonstrated this. In her first session she came to see me because she was "guilty about my past."

I said, "Ok, let's hear about it."

She said, "Don't rush me. I don't know if I can trust you."

I said, "Fair enough."

Erica was in her mid fifties. She was tall and willowy with a hard-life face, but still a beautiful woman who years earlier must have been stunning. She was in her fifth marriage which she pronounced as "great!" She described her husband, a rancher, as "one of the nicest guys who ever lived." They'd been married three years. (I eventually met him. He was one of the nicest guys who ever lived.)

After six sessions I still hadn't heard what she felt guilty about, but she was a very talkative, interesting person with a "rich history." That's analytic-speak for a patient who has had numerous, terrible, life experiences. Erica had been raised in a Catholic orphanage in New York City never knowing her parents. The nuns told her that her parents had been killed in an auto wreck. She had no relatives.

She lived at the orphanage through high school and had no complaints about the experience. She described it as "having twenty mothers—the nuns were good people." She then moved to New Jersey and enrolled in secretarial school. She took dancing lessons at night. In her first class her dance instructor noted her extraordinary talent and through his connections was able to get her an audition for a Broadway play. Erica got the job. "Good thing, too," she laughed, "I couldn't type for shit."

Broadway introduced her to booze, drugs, and unsavory big spenders. She had at least four abortions ("There may have been more. I was wasted for years.") She did time in drunk tanks and suffered an assortment of beatings by her husbands and boyfriends. Sometimes she woke up in places having no idea how she got there. Once she came-to in Los Angeles. Another time in Santa Fe. Rich history. She also met many famous people and for a time was famous herself with her name "up in lights."

That was her life until she checked herself into a re-hab hospital after her fourth divorce. She spent almost one year drying out and "getting my head on straight." She then traveled west to Colorado where she eventually met "Ben," the rancher, and life has been wonderful ever since. Although much of what Erica told me would be guilt producing for many people, this was not the case with her. In the telling of the stories there was much anguish and many tears but no guilt. She blamed her bizarre life in New York City on being drunk, stoned or high.

In the seventh session I decided it was time to ask Erica if she trusted me enough to tell me about that great guilt she carried around, the one she mentioned in our first session. She had been so candid and forthcoming I felt it was safe to bring this up. I was wrong. "Not yet," she said. "I'm in no hurry. What's your hurry?"

By the tenth session, or so, Erica's stories of her past life dried up and she was now telling me about her day to day life on the ranch. She used up an hour describing the calving and branding she and Ben were involved in, another hour on some of the characters who worked on the ranch, another hour on how they'd built an addition to the barn and another one on a recent elk-hunting trip they'd taken on horseback. Interesting stories but hardly the stuff of psychoanalysis. Erica's defenses were not coming down.

Yet she was eager to continue to see me, twice a week, and she was paying full fee. Good for me but not so good for her. I was missing something and decided to take a different tack. I would use my intuition.

My office in Durango had a nice waiting room with comfortable furniture and my consultation room was warm and pleasant. I had a leather chair and ottoman, the patients had either a large, winged back chair or the couch, which was covered with tasteful throws. The walls were adorned with old barnwood siding and there were paintings, weavings and knick-knacks around the room. Although it was in an office complex the entrance to my psychoanalytic office was fairly private. But it was still a psychoanalyst's office and somewhat clinical and intimidating. When Erica arrived for her next session I was waiting for her at the door.

"Do you have to cancel our appointment? Do you have an emergency?" she asked with more than a hint of anxiety and disappointment.

"Not at all. I just feel like getting out of here for a change. Let's take a ride. I'll drive, you talk."

"Oh, okay," she said and happily climbed into my truck. The not-so gifted, uptight psychoanalysts that Freud conned into coming to the U.S. would have been appalled. Patients were not to encounter their analysts outside of the treatment room.

My office was on Florida Road and you may analyze that if you wish. We headed north toward the higher elevations while Erica chatted away about nothing with analytic value. Meanwhile I listened for unconscious clues and got nothing. About ten miles up the road we arrived at Lemon Dam. I parked the truck on top of the dam and turned off the engine. Erica looked out across the water and said, "My god, this is beautiful."

"Yes it is," I agreed. "And this time of year there is a special treat." I told her to look across the lake and above the tree line where a pair of bald eagles were circling. "Oh my god, are those eagles?"

"Yep. We'll sit here awhile and watch them fish. It's fun and you'll be amazed at how inept they are." Moments later one of them dove to the lake's surface, leveled out, and stuck his talons into the water. A fish jumped up right next to him but he missed it and flew back up to join his mate. Then the mate did the same thing, missing her fish also.

"This is great, Jim, I've got to tell Ben about this. Do the eagles ever catch the fish?" I told her they appear to average about one successful attempt out of four. As we sat watching them they didn't make a liar out of me. One out of four.

For the first time since we began seeing each other Erica became silent as we watched the eagles. Many minutes went by before she broke the silence. In a barely audible voice she said, "Jim, I have lied to you and I lied to Ben. I was only on Broadway for five years. After that I quit to be something else." I said nothing.

"Don't you want to know what else?" she asked still at a whisper.

I looked at her, gave her a smile, and said, "I'm in no hurry."

She said, "Touché." Then, looking me right in the eye, and with tears welling up in hers she said, "I was a professional call girl." She buried her face in her hands and sobbed.

We were halfway down the mountain before the tears stopped. I'd said nothing. When she was finally composed, she looked at me and asked, "Will you still continue to see me?"

I could not hold back a guffaw. I twinkled my eyes and said, "Only on one condition. You have to tell me how much you charged. I've always been curious." She punched me, hard, on the arm. (Another rule broken—no physical contact with patients.)

Erica and I spent many more sessions together dealing with her "great guilt." The fact that she had four disastrous marriages, abortions and untold episodes of blacking out from drugs and alcohol did not haunt her. "I never intended for those things to happen, they just did." But being a prostitute, in her mind, was different. "It's what I was, what I chose to be, drunk or sober. That made it different." She had a point.

Erica's problem, in her mind, was how to tell Ben the truth about her past. She loved him and he loved her, "but my lies to him are eating me up with guilt."

"Does he ask you questions about your past?"

"Never."

"Then you're not lying to him so why bring it up?"

"Because it's the right thing to do."

"No, it's not. It's childish and destructive. In other words, it's nuts. It would be a massive undoing of your wonderful life," I said.

I then asked her why she wanted to screw up her marriage with Ben. "He wouldn't leave me because of it," she said defensively.

"Probably not," I agreed. "But it would change things. Ben's a great guy but he's human. And you know it would change things. Hell, it took you a dozen sessions just to tell me. Do not tell him!" I said as strongly as I could—breaking strict analytic rules about giving life advice to patients.

Bless Me, Father, for I Have Sinned

We had that dialogue many times until we traced her need for "complete truth" to the concept of Confession. She had gone to Confession weekly and dutifully for all those years in the orphanage. But, finally, she was able to make the intellectual and emotional distinction between a priest and her husband. "But I always thought you had to be totally honest about everything," she said one day. I told her, in theory, it was best not to tell a specific lie but no one is commanded to tell everything they know, and confess everything they did, except in Confession (and of course, psychoanalysis). The Jesuits, I explained to this long ago Catholic, call this "mental reservation": Don't lie but don't volunteer more than is necessary. She finally got it. We terminated her therapy, and she lived happily ever after with Ben. She really did.

I don't know how long Erica and I would have been together before she admitted her great guilt had I not taken her to see the eagles. Being out of the artificial setting of the office and seeing me more as a whole person than as a professional lessened her defenses. Before Erica I had only taken children and adolescent patients on the ride to Lemon Dam, but after my experience with her I occasionally took other adults. The eagles seemed to free them up, also.

All professions have rules that sometimes need to be altered. Letting Erica see me in a normal setting—out of the office and driving my truck—was helpful to her. Also, she was not a "psychoanalytic case." Smart as she was intellectually, she was essentially devoid of insight. I never suggested she lie down on the couch because it would have scared her to death and she'd have fled. Also, I did not want to psychoanalyze her. She was fifty-five years old, had led the cruelest of lives and had finally found happiness. Why mess around with that?

I could have convinced Erica to continue treatment but did not. Too risky. If we had unearthed her deep feelings which accompanied her horrible past, there is no telling where it would have taken us. Emotionally she was a very fragile person. "Letting her be" was the thing my gut said to do. In-depth psychoanalysis is not for everybody.

And not only did I not psychoanalyze Erica, I only gingerly conducted psychotherapy with her. Our time together could best be described as "psychotherapy-ultralite." Mostly I became her surrogate priest and she was a penitent for the longest of Confessions. This was a therapeutic experience for her—but not to any depth. Confession is great for the soul but has no lasting effects on someone's unconscious psychic dynamics. We barely touched her unconscious mind, and I'm glad we didn't. She'd found Ben and happiness on her own. All I did was convince her not to screw it up. A trusted friend could have done the same thing.

16

Sometimes We
Make Mistakes

Of Course

Shrinks, like other professionals, are a kaleidoscope of humanity. They are fat, skinny, tall, short, handsome, beautiful, ugly. Some have bombastic personalities and others are terribly shy. If there is a common thread, and of course there is, shrinks, like their patients, knew they weren't quite right. That's why they entered the mental health field. Psychoanalysis has been called the only profession where people pay you so you can cure yourself.

When we choose a profession it is our powerful unconscious minds that are doing the choosing, often utilizing the defense mechanism known as *counterphobia.* This simply means we are unconsciously frightened by something and to counter that fear we incorporate it into our lives and put a positive spin on it. Following are psychoanalytic truisms about chosen careers that often have merit: pilots are afraid of heights; schoolteachers were traumatized as students; medical doctors are hypochondriacs; nurses want to be nursed; lawyers grew up with too many (or not enough) laws; salesmen are insecure; clergy know they are basically flawed people. There's a fine line between the cop and the robber, the fireman and the firebug. Jean Rosenbaum told a story about meeting the famous producer and director Mel Brooks in the Green Room before appearing on *The Tonight Show.* (Rosenbaum was touting a book he'd written.) When Brooks learned Jean was a psychiatrist, he said, "Tell me, Doctor, isn't *everything* in life counterphobic?"

16. Sometimes We Make Mistakes: Of Course

A psychoanalyst's job is to "make right," to put some kind of order into the ten thousand-piece jigsaw puzzle of ironical, paradoxical and conflicting emotions we carry around and *we practitioners must begin with ourselves*. When Freud was training analysts he did not spend a lot of time with them. Six days a week for a couple months and they were on their own. So they got a feel for the basics and dynamics of the discipline but did not experience its depth. He encouraged them to continue their personal analysis. The story is told about two of Freud's newly trained analysts who were practicing on each other. The one lying on the couch said something which prompted the other in the chair to make an interpretation. It was way off the mark. The one on the couch said, "That was really stupid. You're a lot more fucked up than me." The one in the chair said, "I think you're right. Let's trade places." And they did. Psychotherapists today are highly trained, especially the heavy-duty psychoanalysts who undergo years of personal analysis. But all of us are human and can indeed make mistakes.

Our mental health institute in the Midwest held weekly seminars where cases were discussed. Psychoanalysts and therapists took turns presenting their cases in order to teach the students and to get feedback from other therapists. These sessions were lively, informative, good for the therapists and, therefore, good for the patients. The patients' real names were never used, to protect their privacy. I will never forget one of these cases related by one of the institute's most experienced analysts. The presenting symptom ("I came to see you because…") was a marriage problem.

"Elizabeth's" husband's occupation was in a prestigious profession but one that did not, and never would, pay well. But he was devoted to it, and was very happy in his work. When Elizabeth married "Jerry" she knew that riches would never be theirs, but that was four years ago. Now she wanted out. "I want nice things and a bigger house," she told her therapist. "All our friends are getting big raises and moving to the suburbs. We're stuck in the city and will never go anywhere but Jerry won't consider changing careers. It isn't fair!" When a patient uses the expression "It isn't fair" the first thing therapists say to themselves is: "Oh shit. A five-year-old."

And Elizabeth had numerous other complaints: "I think Jerry loves

Mary (their dog) more than me. He spends more time with her than me. He used to take me out to dinner and dancing but now he rarely takes me anywhere because he tells me it's too expensive. I want him to take me on a cruise to Hawaii, but he told me it's out of the question. He says, 'You know we couldn't afford that.' Sometimes he has to go to work on Saturday and leaves me home alone. He never brings me surprise gifts anymore. He used to bring me gifts all the time but that ended years ago."

Elizabeth's marital complaints were seemingly endless, but by the third session her shrink was able to begin getting her personal history. An only child, Elizabeth was doted upon. Her father was an engineer and her mother did not work out of the home. They were not wealthy but lack of money was not an issue. They lived in a large house in an upscale suburb. When she went away to college, her parents gave her a new car and paid all her college expenses. She described her parents' marriage as "romantic and stable," expressions we don't hear often.

Elizabeth and Jerry met in college and soon after graduation they married. "I guess I knew his career choice wouldn't pay much but I didn't care then. I was young and he loved me. Now he doesn't love me and I want a divorce," she said, daintily dabbing a tear from her eye. Elizabeth's therapist sensed there was more to her story than the lack of money. He was also put off by Elizabeth's "me-me and I-I" talk. Psychotherapy is the most narcissistic of experiences, and we expect to hear lots of "me-me's and I-I's," but Elizabeth had taken it to a new level.

During the fourth session the therapist felt comfortable enough to inquire into Jerry and Elizabeth's sex life, and that's when Elizabeth dropped the bomb. "I hate our sex life and I always have." The therapist figured he would now get to the real reason for Elizabeth's wish to get out of the marriage. Perhaps Jerry was kinky in his sexual demands or maybe Elizabeth had found a better lover, or perhaps she didn't like sex. Some people simply don't like sex but concoct seemingly logical reasons for their dislike. The therapist was about to hear one of these reasons. "What's wrong with your sex life?" he asked.

"Jerry's penis is enormous," Elizabeth explained, "you should see it! He hurts me terribly when he puts it in me. I hate it! That's why we don't have kids. We quit having regular sex years ago. I just jack him off. It's not normal for married people to live like that."

Elizabeth was about 5 feet 8 inches tall and possessed the normal curvature of a woman. When asked to describe Jerry, she said he was 5 feet 6 inches tall, "skinny as a rail," and reiterated he had the biggest male member she'd ever seen.

"How many penises have you seen?" was the obvious question from the therapist.

"Just Jerry's. I was a virgin when we married. But I have seen pictures and statues," she explained." And he's way bigger than any of them. He's even bigger than those guys in X-rated movies. He brings those movies home to try to get me horny. They disgust me."

At this juncture in the therapy Elizabeth's analyst decided to present this case at a training seminar. After we had heard the details it was unanimously decided that: (A) We should get Jerry in to see a therapist to get his side of the story, if he would consent to this. He did, and another analyst, "Bruce," was assigned to see him. (B) Elizabeth sounded like an infantile character in many ways. Not only did she grossly overuse the words "me and I" but her affect was pouty, and when she talked she ended every sentence on a high note making it sound like a question. She was an attractive woman but this valley girl form of speech gave her the affect of a whiny child. We also agreed that her complaint about the size of Jerry's penis was, no doubt, an exaggeration.

Bruce began to see Jerry and liked him immediately. He was bright, funny, dedicated to his profession, and terribly concerned about the state of his marriage. He told Bruce that he loved his wife, even though she was never happy anymore. He said he'd do whatever he could to make the marriage work. Bruce reported this to the group and added that Jerry was, indeed, slight of statue.

Diplomacy is necessary when inquiring about patients' genitalia, so Bruce waited until trust was firmly established before he broached the topic with Jerry. Elizabeth and Jerry had given the therapists permission to discuss specific details from each other's sessions when they felt it would be a benefit to the other person, or the marriage. One day Bruce asked him about the size of his penis, telling him that Elizabeth told her therapist it was quite large and it hurt her when he penetrated her.

"She has always said that," he said, "but it is not true. I've been in the Army and plenty of locker rooms. I know my dick is only slightly bigger than average. Elizabeth doesn't like sex and never has. I think she's frigid and uses that as an excuse."

Bruce asked if other women had mentioned it, and he said there had never been another woman. He, too, was a virgin when he married.

Unfortunately Elizabeth and Jerry didn't make it. After a few months of therapy, they divorced. Jerry was devastated. Elizabeth was relieved. Elizabeth terminated her therapy but Jerry continued seeing Bruce as they put his new life together. He had been crushed by his failed marriage, but he eventually regained his self-esteem and sense of humor. Bruce reported to our group that he had no doubt Jerry would have become whole again, over time, without the aid of psychotherapy. (One aspect of therapy is that it hurries this process.) Within a year Jerry had an active social life. His sense of humor and overall positive outlook made him an appealing person in the singles scene. His therapy terminated.

There are approximately six million people in the Chicago area. A few months later in a singles bar, Jerry met "Catherine" who was, incredibly, one of Bruce's patients. "Bruce, you're not going to believe who I met last night," she gushed as the session began. She told him she'd met a former patient of his, a guy named Jerry. She said that they really liked each other and had plans for the following weekend. That weekend went great and Catherine was thrilled with her new boyfriend. "He's so funny! We laugh all the time," she gushed. But when she arrived at her next session Catherine was anything but her usually chipper self. "What's wrong?" Bruce asked.

She told him that when she and Jerry checked into a motel and started making out he was gentle and loving and did all the right things, but when they got naked she was shocked. "As you know I have been with many men but I have never seen anything like this guy's dick!" She said Jerry was built like a horse and they'd have no future. "Sex with him hurts!" Bruce could hardly wait for the next seminar to tell us the news. We had really screwed up.

126

Damn It!

While we're on the topic of screwing up I'll tell you about a time I made a mistake with a patient. I'm still ashamed of myself and embarrassed by it.

My patient, "Mark," was an attorney in his late twenties. His wife had recently filed for divorce and he was devastated. They had only been married eight months. It was Mark's first marriage but his wife's second. She had two daughters whom Mark had legally adopted. Mark had no clue his marriage was ending until he was served with divorce papers at his law office. He immediately called his home and the maid said that his wife, kids, and "some man" had left in the man's car. Mark learned the "man" was his wife's first husband.

A friend of Mark's advised him to come see me. He was unable to work, sleep, or think about anything except the loss of his family. He'd quit shaving, wore the same clothes and showered, I noted, infrequently. Our sessions consisted of Mark expressing his disbelief at what happened to him and his bewilderment at his wife's behavior. "I had no idea what was going on. Not once did she tell me she was unhappy with me. We could have talked it out. I know we could have. What am I going to do? Oh God, oh God, Please help me!" Then he'd break down sobbing.

After three sessions of essentially the same dynamics I was getting frustrated and decided to intervene. One of the most important things people should do when they feel they have been wrongly treated is to express anger at the person who hurt them. In our few sessions I had suggested to Mark that he must be feeling anger at his wife but he would hear none of that. "No, no," he wailed, "It must be my fault! I must have done something to offend Jesus and that's why she left me!"

Mark was an exceptionally religious person. In his mind all elements of life were controlled by God. He firmly believed if someone stayed on the square with God his life would be smooth sailing. Hard to understand that an intelligent, educated person would believe that (especially a lawyer), but Mark did.

During the fourth session Mark was continuing to blame himself for his misery, because he had unknowingly sinned against Jesus—and I had heard enough. It was time, I thought, for him to quit wallowing

127

in guilt and self-pity and to start getting some perspective. I blithely said to him, "Mark, that is absolute nonsense. Jesus didn't do this to you."

His head jerked up and he looked at me. I think it was the first thing I said to him that he actually heard. His eyes got huge as he stared at me and his mouth started moving but no words came out, only guttural sounds. He put his head down, gripped the arms of the chair then looked back up at me—eyes still agape. "You, you Jew atheist!" he said, "I should have known better than to come here. All I had left was my religion and you just tried to take it away!"

I was stunned. "Mark, I'm no atheist, I'm a Christian like you," I said breaking at least one rule of analysis. "I just don't believe Jesus had anything to do with your wife leaving. You're a good man. You were a good husband. You adopted your wife's kids. You should not be blaming yourself."

He did not hear me, because of my impatience, arrogance, and flipness, Mark's therapy had just become a disaster. I had grossly underestimated his fragility and how dare I question his religious beliefs? I was the one who had sinned, against my profession.

"Send me your bill," he said as he walked out of the office. "I won't be coming back."

I have relived that session dozens of times over the years always arriving at the same conclusion: Mark needed to wallow in self-pity longer than I was willing to let him and the thing holding him together was his faith, not me, the narcissistic analyst. I should have realized this and kept my big mouth shut.

Yes, sometimes we make mistakes.

17

Big Boys Don't Cry

Men Do

I was sitting in the rocking chair on the front porch of our house in the North Carolina mountains enjoying the summer night. Barbara was out of town visiting her parents. It was an extraordinarily pleasant evening with soft breezes and a light rain. The insects in the trees had begun their eternal argument about Katie: "She did ... She didn't! ... Yes, she did ... No, she didn't!"

With one sip left in my nightcap, I was thinking of fixing another to extend the beautiful evening when the phone rang. In the deepest of Southern accents, a man asked if I was the James Joyce who wrote the book about flying helicopters in Vietnam. He'd read a review of it in the newspaper. I told him I was.

"I flew choppers there, too," he said. "Do you got time to talk to me? Am ah botherin' you? Should ah call back 'nother time?"

I said I'd be happy to talk to him and asked the standard Vietnam questions: What years were you there, and what unit did you serve with?

In no time we discovered we had mutual acquaintances, had very similar experiences, and had even served in the same battalion although at different times. A camaraderie was swiftly established. He'd had two tours in Vietnam, had been shot down three times, and could count forty friends who'd been killed there. He went from story to story, obviously needing to talk. I simply listened. Then there was a long pause, and when he spoke again it was barely above a whisper.

"You ever been to that wall?" Knowing he meant the Vietnam

Memorial in Washington, D.C., I told him that I had. Another long pause.

"Did you break down?" he asked quietly.

"Yes," I said, "I did."

Another pause. "I figure I would, too, so I ain't gonna go see it. Ah don't want ma wife to see me cryun.'"

Soon after this we hung up. He said he was going to buy my book. I asked him to call me after he'd read it. I went into the house, fixed that second nightcap, returned to the porch, and thought about our conversation. I no longer heard the owl, the insects, or the rain. I lost friends in Vietnam, too. I started cryun.

Veryl, my first analyst, had been told by my ex-wife that I was a Vietnam veteran. Early in my personal analysis she asked about it: "Did your experiences in Vietnam affect you in any way?"

"No, not at all," I said.

"Surely it changed your life at least a little," she countered.

"I don't think so," I countered back. "I was only there a year and I wasn't a hero. I just did my job and came home."

"But you flew helicopters—you must have seen some terrible things," she persisted.

"Thousands of guys flew helicopters. The guys that got the worst of it were the infantry soldiers on the ground," I said, and meant it.

"Okay," she said, obviously not believing me. "But it's hard to imagine the war didn't have some impact on you. Maybe we'll come back to it."

We never did get back to it.

Three decades later we had a Joyce family reunion. On that same front porch my nephews from California started asking questions about my time in Vietnam. I was happy to answer them. I was not like many vets who won't, or can't, talk about their time in combat. I told them story after story, but then got to one I couldn't finish. This had never happened. My eyes filled with tears and my throat constricted and I excused myself. I went into the house and poured a double scotch.

Part of my job as a helicopter pilot was flying troops (twenty-year-old kids) into battle. It was a godawful time for them and for us pilots. Seeing the fresh, eager faces of my nephews reminded me of those troops, and those memories flooded my eyes. So yes, Veryl, my Vietnam experiences did have an impact on me, a whole book's worth, but it took unexpected tears to finally get it out of me—thirty-five years later. Like I said, no one is completely psychoanalyzed.

Crying, even in this enlightened age of psychological awareness, is still a problem for many men. It is a blatant showing of emotions, which they consider to be in the female realm. Because females are the "weaker sex" crying is, therefore, a sign of weakness in these men's minds. When I was growing up the crying issue was clearly explained to me by my two-fisted, Irish father. He left no confusion in my mind. He stated, often, the way it was supposed to be: "Women cry outside and men cry inside," and that settled that. After the age of seven or so, I recall crying only two other times. The first time was at age twelve when my grandfather died and the other time was at age twenty-nine when my father died. Sorry, Dad, I couldn't help it.

The Worst

I wasn't a crier on the outside until I found myself in psychoanalysis and then the tears flowed freely, especially at the beginning. Early on in my analysis it became painfully clear that our marriage was over. I cried for myself, of course, but I cried for the dead marriage, also. It had had its own life and identity. I cried for lost hopes, dreams, plottings and plannings that would never come to be. And I cried for the past. Much of it had just become a lie. But the greatest pain came from knowing I would soon lose my boys, now ages six and seven. When the divorce was final they would be accompanying their mother back to Florida. I would remain in Colorado to finish my training.

Our last night together as a family, so to speak, was in Albuquerque, New Mexico. We went out to dinner and then it was time for good-bye. The next day they'd be leaving. I kissed the boys and climbed into my pickup truck to return to Durango, a four-hour drive. I was not out of the restaurant parking lot before a scream of anguish came out of me. And then another scream, and another, as the finality of what was happening sank in. Tears gushed from my eyes and the screams kept coming and this scream-cry continued as I drove across the New Mexico desert. I could not contain it and could barely see the road. After an hour I stopped in the beat-up little town of Cuba, near the Apache Reservation. I composed myself long enough to check into a run-down motel, then found a liquor store and bought a quart of vodka. I returned to the room and drank the whole thing, all the while weeping in disbelief. It was the worst goddamned night of my life.

When I entered psychoanalysis and my marriage fell apart I made up for all the crying I didn't do as a teen and young adult. I've been pretty good at crying ever since. Now I have to tell on myself. After the divorce I continued my personal psychoanalysis and was seeing patients under supervision when my boys came to visit the following summer. We were driving down Durango's Main Street when I asked where they wanted to go for lunch. Jim said, "McDonald's." Walter said, "Burger King." I said, "Well we're not going to both and McDonald's is closer so we'll go there." Walter started crying, which really pissed me off. I said, "Shut up, damn it. Boys don't cry!" A second later I could have cut my tongue out. All that analysis and training and I was still under the influence of my dad!

I apologized to Walter, we went to both places, and I, Mr. Shrink the Expert, demonstrated I was less than astute as a parent and still had work to do as a patient. I should not have given my sons an option. Of course, they'd say different places. I shouldn't have yelled at Walter and certainly shouldn't have told him not to cry. I also should not have given in, and gone to both places. And I should not have told Jim to wipe that smug look off his face, before I smacked it off. This is getting embarrassing. Let's get out of this story.

Typical patients in psychotherapy are between thirty and forty-five years of age and most of them (I'd guess seventy-five percent) are women. Women are generally good at crying and are usually easier to treat because they are closer to their emotions than men and are not, therefore, afraid of them. Women's biological make-up is more circular than men's and so, too, is their psychological make-up. Their intellects and emotions touch more often, hanging around together like friends. We men, on the other hand, are linear in nature and like to keep our emotions behind us as we stridently go forth. To get men to stop and wait for their feelings to catch up presents a challenge to a therapist.

Psychotherapy must be a combination of thought and feeling with neither, alone, contributing much to eventual well-being. They must be integrated so when a memory gives up a sad time from the past, or life is currently wretched, the patient should intellectually know it, emotionally feel it—and cry. It is good for him and no shrink's office is without a box of Kleenex. It is a tool of our trade. We can write off the purchase on our income tax.

I had a patient we'll call "Grady." He was a huge man, 6 feet 5 inches tall, and almost 300 pounds. He came to see me because he had suddenly found himself a single parent—the father of two girls ages two and six. His wife had run off with another woman. He wanted to "do right by" his daughters in his new-found role. Grady knew they would be "fucked up" by their mother leaving. He came for advice, not psychoanalysis, he said.

I asked him some details about his failed marriage and he took much of the blame. He worked as a sales representative and his job kept him away from home for weeks at a time. He was full of remorse. He was also terribly embarrassed by his wife's departure with a woman. "How did I turn her into a queer?" he wanted to know.

"You didn't," I told him.

As we talked it became clear that his main fear, and the reason he came to see me, was that he would "raise my girls to be lesbian." I told him we'd work to be sure that didn't happen but for now we'd concentrate on him.

"How are you coping with your guilt and hurt?" I asked

He smiled and said, "I drink a lot."

"Have you been able to cry about it?" I asked.

"Fuck no, I don't cry."

"Why not?"

"Because men don't cry."

"That's bullshit," I said. "Your life is a disaster, you have every reason to cry."

He looked at me like I'd just said the most profound thing he'd ever heard. His eyes welled up, he put his hands to his face and began to sob. "Go for it, Grady," I said softly. "It's okay."

He cried for five minutes or so and when he finished he gave me an embarrassed smile. "That's the first time I cried since I was a kid," he said wiping his eyes. "Thanks for telling me it was okay."

I've heard people say (I've said it myself) that they are afraid to cry because once they start they may not be able to stop. This is an honest fear, albeit neurotic. No one can cry forever, so go for it man … and take your time.

18

The Safe Haven

INT

Many of my patients were suffering from depression. Some were especially down in the dumps and others were only vaguely sad—but all the time. Depression is now at the epidemic level in the United States and I'd like to give a plug to the pharmaceutical industry. Through years of research and development it has discovered numerous drugs that effectively alter moods so that people can get out of bed, go to work, adequately function within their families and cope from day to day. These drugs do not "cure" depression or other emotional problems but they may keep them from overwhelming. So "Attaboy" to the drug companies from a traditional psychoanalyst. They are filling a necessary need, and we'll talk more about them in Chapter 25.

Numerous events and circumstances can cause depression, but often at the root will be anger (here it is again) turned against the self. We don't feel this anger as anger, because it is in the unconscious. When it emerges into consciousness it is disguised—similar to the real meaning of a dream—and can take a variety of forms including obesity and other oral fixations, feelings of malaise, weepiness, hopelessness, exhaustion, listlessness, helplessness, worthlessness, frustration and, if serious enough, the wish to self-destruct.

Let me tell you about "Karl." His primary residence was an estate on a waterfront canal in Fort Lauderdale, Florida. His sixty-foot yacht was docked behind the house. Karl and his family enjoyed watching the large, beautiful cruise ships coming and going from Port Everglades as they majestically passed by the family's back yard. He also had a second home in the Colorado mountains. Everything he owned was mortgage free. Karl's wife loved him and he loved her. They had three happy, healthy kids. Life couldn't be better.

During our first session, Karl told me that after graduating from college he had an idea to make money in the emerging computer business. He borrowed $5,000 as start-up capital and lived a Spartan existence while he got his idea up and running. Before long he was able to hire an assistant and then another and another. Within five years Karl's company had five hundred employees and went public. Ten years later he sold his shares to a Fortune 100 company for over $1 billion. He was 33. He remained with his company working as a consultant for two more years and then fully retired. Karl's life embodied the American dream. He told me he was thinking of killing himself.

Karl was a very bright guy, formally educated in the finest of schools, and wise to the ways of the world. He knew, consciously, how fortunate he was, yet it made no difference in his mind. "I see no purpose in life, Jim. It's all going to end anyway, why wait for it?"

Applying logic, reason and common sense to Karl's suicidal thoughts would get us nowhere but I pointed out, of course, that if he killed himself it would be devastating to his wife, kids and other loved ones. Karl, of course, knew this. I also could have pointed out to him that he had more to be thankful for than almost anyone who ever lived; that he should be ashamed of himself for being depressed; that he should get on his knees and thank God for all he'd been given and that he should pull himself up by his bootstraps, put a smile on his face and get the hell out of my office. He then would have killed himself for sure.

One of the nice things about being a shrink is knowing that when a person is as screwed up as Karl, the cause of the condition almost invariably goes back to his childhood and can be ferreted out. He was not terminally ill nor was there a serious illness of a person dear to him; his finances couldn't be better; he was not on his way to prison for fraud; he loved his family and they loved him; his name had not been in the newspaper for doing something embarrassing or dastardly. Life had not been cruel to him as an adult, just the opposite. The self-destructive feelings must come from an early time. They did not come from something he ate. I explained this to him.

It's a good idea to talk to potential suicides in the most candid of ways. They need something to grab onto, even if it sounds like nonsense, and Karl's coming to see me of his own volition was a positive sign. I had not talked him off of a ledge.

When I told Karl that his feelings of hopelessness probably came from his childhood it sounded foolish to him and he said so. I agreed with him that it sounded foolish. I told him he would have to trust me and that I wanted to know every single detail he could recall from his childhood beginning with his first memory. Skeptical as he was, he began talking.

Karl was raised in a small city in the South. His father had been an insurance broker and his mother an accountant. Karl excelled in school and earned an academic scholarship to an Ivy League college. His first memory was at his grandparents' home playing on the front porch with his younger brother, his older sister, and "a whole bunch of cousins." His mother was on the swing with his grandmother, his dad and uncles were pitching horseshoes in the yard. Norman Rockwell couldn't have painted a more pleasant picture.

I learned that his folks had few arguments, were affectionate with each other, and were still alive, having recently celebrated their sixtieth wedding anniversary. They were now living at the old homestead of his grandparents. I also learned that Karl's depression, which had intermittently plagued him since his early twenties, had become particularly severe of late. His first serious thought of suicide began two months before entering therapy, shortly after his parents' anniversary celebration weekend. "Okay, let's hear about the weekend," I said, "then we'll get back to your childhood."

"I made the mistake of going to the river," he said. "I thought it might be good for me but it made me feel even worse."

"What river?"

"Where my brother drowned," he said, as though I knew about his brother. Karl was already transferring on me, as if I was a parent, assuming that I knew all about him. This was our fourth session and I'd not heard about his brother.

"What happened?" I asked and Karl related the story. He and his brother had wandered away from the grandparents' house to the banks of a rapidly running stream. His little brother had fallen into it and was swept away.

"How old were you?" I asked.

"I was four and my brother was three," he answered as his chin quivered. "I'm responsible for his death."

I asked Karl to tell me everything he remembered about this awful event. He didn't remember any details except his brother calling out to him as he was carried downstream.

Karl and I worked together for a year or so as he recovered from his depression. My mission was to get this intelligent man to realize that four-year-olds are not responsible people. This led us to the obvious question: Who was supposed to be watching his brother and him? Children three and four years old should not be allowed to wander, especially if there's water nearby. He did recall that his devastated parents told him he was not to blame for his brother's death and they loved him. They also made him promise never to talk about it and to get it out of his mind. With such advice these well-meaning, naïve people planted a time bomb in Karl. Fortunately we were able to defuse it. His anger could now be properly vented at those negligent adults who allowed (caused) the tragedy.

Karl's depression was an easy one to remedy because it was directly linked to an isolated event. Most causes of depression are not so pure and are the result of unfair treatment, attitudes, or inconsistencies stretching across many years. This kind of background is much more difficult to deal with than a single traumatic event. It is ambivalent and we hear words like: "Yes, but; on the other hand; sometimes; not always; maybe; only when they are drinking, etc." Inconsistencies lead to ambivalence that torques the mind. Strangely, a child is better off having a parent who is consistently mean or negligent rather than having one who bounces from angel to devil.

Naturally, there has never been a completely consistent parent, so we make allowances for the occasional lapse and, paradoxically, an occasional inconsistency may help to build character. "Frustration in childhood equals character in adulthood," is an old saying with merit. But when parents are consistently inconsistent, emotional problems in their offspring will result.

Let 'er rip, Louise

Perhaps the toughest cases to treat are patients from families where there is *nothing* going on. "Louise" was a thirty-one years old, married with two children, a boy and a girl, ages one and two respectively. She was married to "David," a fast rising executive in a large stock brokerage firm. They had been married eight years. Louise described her marriage as "very good." Both were college graduates. They shared the same Jewish faith and attended synagogue on a regular basis. They had no health or financial problems. Louise was an attractive woman; David was a handsome man. They were the perfect young family except for one thing— Louise was no longer able to function. Getting out of bed was an effort, getting dressed was a challenge, doing any sort of household chore sapped her energy in minutes and she went back to bed. She spent most of her waking hours weeping. She was not consciously entertaining thoughts of suicide but told me in our first session that if she died it would probably be best for her family.

"I want to get better but I don't even remember what it's like to feel good. I am worthless and I've lost all hope," she said, crying softly. Louise, like Karl, was depressed for no apparent reason.

David, who drove his wife to her first session, was the catalyst for her being there. He said they'd had been to numerous medical doctors who could find nothing wrong with Louise. The last one suggested psychotherapy. "What have I done wrong?" he asked in a brief meeting after the session.

"I doubt you've done anything wrong," I told him.

We agreed Louise would see me the next day and then three times a week for the foreseeable future. "Be patient and understanding," I said. "She will get better." His relief was palpable.

Some would say I went too far in assuring David his wife would get better. After all, in only fifty minutes I knew practically nothing about Louise and the dynamics of her life. But I felt very comfortable making that assurance because Louise had not yet sunk to the level of being non-conversant. She was motivated to get better and, by now, many years into the profession, I had seen dozens and dozens of depressed patients. They all got better—after I figured out what I was doing.

The Mind and I

The next day Louise and I went to work, beginning in the recent past. She told me she first sensed her depression about six months after her second child, the boy, was born. She was bathing him, a fun time for both of them with "big sister" helping, when Louise had an image of her little boy becoming a man.

"I saw his face getting older and older and then I saw him as an old man dead in a casket. I broke out crying, the kids freaked out. God, I'm embarrassed to tell you this," she said. "How could I have such terrible vision, fantasy, or whatever it was? I made my darling little boy an old man and killed him off! God, that is so sick!" she exclaimed, "How could I do that?"

This was not a rhetorical question. She was looking directly into my eyes and she wanted an answer. "That's an easy one, Louise," I said pausing for emphasis. Then I smiled and said, "The mind is a terrible thing to have." She looked at me like I was nuts, then thought about it for a second and laughed out loud.

Everyone has terrible thoughts from time to time, although most won't admit to them. I told her I had a male patient once who confessed, with great shame, that in church he observed the women and wondered how many of them he could have an affair with. He fantasized about them throughout the service. He was certain he was going to hell. She laughed at that, also. Then I told her of another patient who kept having the fantasy of her ex-spouse being hit by a train. Louise liked that one, too, and I assured her once again that evil, dastardly thoughts were not only common, but quite normal. They, like dreams, are psychic release mechanisms.

I explained to her that no matter how much she loved her little boy, and would never really hurt him, there was a part of her, buried in the unconscious, that wanted him out of her life. She gave me a strange look but did not protest.

"For instance," I continued, "babies are a lot of work, their needs are many and sometimes seem insatiable. You also have a toddler, your little girl, who is no doubt a handful and who is jealous of her brother. Both kids are in diapers. I wouldn't be surprised if you missed the alone time you had with your daughter, just the two of you, which you'll never have again. Babies wreck your sex life for a multitude of reasons. Lots of other things could make you wish the baby would go away, so your unconscious mind bumped him off. Naturally you'd never do it, but there's no harm in thinking about it. As a matter of fact it's good for you."

So far I had been doing much of the talking. This dynamic would end shortly, but at the beginning of therapy a patient should be made comfortable with the fact that a shrink is not a judgmental "tsk tsking" parent. As quickly as possible the patient should realize the analyst not only understands "evil" thoughts but has them himself. I told her one of my kids had been an incessant crier who had colic for over a year. I used to fantasize throwing him out the window. (She really liked that one.) Candidness from therapists alleviates the natural defenses patients bring into a session and makes it very clear they are there to be understood, not judged.

One of the first things patients learn when they come to analysis is that their unpleasant thoughts and fantasies are not only normal but are also universal. Show me a person who hasn't secretly wished, at least a few times, that he (or she) could be free of their spouses and their kids and start all over again. Show me the person who has not wished someone close to them would lose their job, instead of getting the big promotion. Who among us isn't jealous of those who inherit their wealth instead of earning it themselves? Who hasn't secretly wished the boss would have a coronary so we could get his job? People hate it when a sibling makes more money than them, gets more acclaim, marries better. To deny these dastardly thoughts is dangerous to emotional health. It's the unconscious talking, the little kid "id," and to think such thoughts are evil, psychologically speaking, is silly.

One of the great fallacies of our Western culture is the concept that "to think something evil is just as bad as doing it," the "lusting in your heart" business. This is not only nonsense, it can be crippling to the mind. It wasn't until the Second Vatican Council in the 1960s that the church finally proclaimed there's a real difference between thinking about doing something bad and actually doing it. That corrective dictum has yet to penetrate our Christian Western psyche, however, including Catholics. The "think it" stuff has been around too long and still produces enormous, neurotic guilt.

Louise's depression seemed to begin when she had her second baby, but as we took a closer look it became clear there'd been evidence of it for many years, though not in its current severity. She said there were times in her life when she was happy, "But they never lasted very long." When people asked her, in a friendly way, "How are you doing?" her reply was either, "Okay, I guess" or "pretty good." It was never "Great!" *Joi de vivre* never applied to Louise.

Naturally I was most interested in her early years to see if there had been specific trauma such as physical or sexual abuse, or the death of someone dear to her, but there had not. She had two siblings, a brother two years older and a sister two years younger. To this day, and as far back as she could remember, she felt close to them. Next we tackled her parents to see how they may have contributed to her lifelong semi-sad state, now culminating in intense depression.

Louise described her dad as a "nice enough man" but also as "sort of cold." He was an administrator for a government agency and had attained moderate success. He never laughed out loud and rarely smiled. He wanted everything, and everybody, to be "just so." He lived by a thousand rules—the proper times to eat, go to bed, get up. His clothing was impeccable, his desk was compulsively neat; he got his hair cut every two weeks at the same time, on the same day, by the same barber.

"Dad didn't like change or surprises," she said. "I guess he was the perfect bureaucrat. And, oh, he never kissed us and only lately has he been able to give us kids a hug but there's no emotion in it. But he never laid a hand on us in anger. Whenever we'd do something he disapproved of he would withdraw even more into himself and not speak to us—sometimes for days. That really hurt."

Louise then described her mother. "She, like my dad, was not affectionate with us kids. Hugs and kisses were not part of our growing up. At the same time Mom did all the right things. She washed and ironed our clothes, prepared good meals, cared for us when we were sick, drove us wherever we needed to go. In a way she was a perfect mom in the things she did, but none of us felt close to her. It's like she was acting at being a mom but not really feeling it or, now that I think about it, I'm not sure she wanted to be a mother."

Louise had just described two emotionally depressed people. No wonder Louise was down in the dumps. Her childhood taught her the way parents are supposed to be—without joy. Louise's parents went through life "by the numbers," robotic towards each other and toward their children.

Louise was a tough case because the sources of her depression were subtle. Frequent causes like a broken home or sexual or physical abuses were not there. Even the emotional background seemed fine, at first. There'd been no screaming, fighting, crying or throwing of objects. No one was a drunk. On the other hand there'd been no laughter either. The more Louise talked, the more she realized there'd been nothing on the emotional upside in her childhood home.

When we say that environmental factors can cause emotional illness people think we mean specific events, and certainly that may be the case. But the *mood in the home* is also a contributor, perhaps the strongest, and every home has a mood. Homes can be anxious, dreary, fearful, suspicious, contentious, contemptuous, spiteful, overly competitive, gloomy, tense, et al. These negative moods create the atmosphere that is incorporated into the developing minds of kids. This was at the heart of Louise's depression. She grew up in a home that was devoid of joy and laughter. Therefore life, to her, was a serious, sad business.

Louise was a motivated patient because somewhere along the way she determined that she wanted her kids to love life, not to merely exist in it the way she had been programmed. But to pass this legacy to them she would have to love life first. Louise and I were together over three years. During that time she did lots of yelling and crying and, of course, laughing. In the safe house of therapy she could be a whole human being and say anything "I fucking well want to say." She learned early on that I would not be shocked, appalled, or judgmental. Her psychotherapy provided Louise a truly corrective emotional experience. For the first time in her life she felt free to say whatever came into her mind no matter how "evil" it was.

Many people, including professionals, believe that depression and other mental illnesses are hereditary like skin tone, eye color and shape of ears. They think it's a biological condition. I don't think so in most cases. I don't believe there's a gene for depression anymore than there's a gene for joy. Mental illness is sort of hereditary, however, in that depressed parents are more likely to raise depressed kids. Being joyful towards life is a learned response. So, too, is seeing it as drudgery.

One of my first patients, "Suzanne," a woman in her late fifties, gave me my first hard look at what it felt like to be depressed. During our first session, without a trace of emotion, she matter-of-factly stated, "I want to die and I wish I had the guts to kill myself but I don't, so I'll just have to wait for it to happen naturally. And I hope there is no such thing as an after-life. I want to cease to exist." (Yikes.)

Part of Suzanne's depression stemmed from a teenage pregnancy. She'd carried the baby to term but was forced by her parents to give it up. She never saw the child. "They wouldn't even tell me if it was a boy or girl." She said she felt like someone had reached inside of her, grabbed her soul, and ripped it out.

Losing an infant, the death of a sibling or having parents with flat, oppressive affects caused depression in Suzanne, Karl, and Louise, but there are a multitude of other causes. If they are not obviously from present circumstances then into childhood we must go. When someone loses someone, or something, dear to them, or experiences serious illness, depression is a natural emotion. There is a tangible, current reason for this kind of sorrow and it is appropriate. But it will also go away in time. Chronic depression must be treated.

Suicide

Depression is a step to suicide, of course, and losing a patient to suicide is a psychotherapist's greatest fear. Normally we are aware when a patient is a potential suicide and can deal with it. If it takes two sessions per day, and phone calls in between, the terrible wish can be talked out. Also, medication is certainly advised. But if the patient gives no clues we can indeed be fooled. There was a case in a psychiatric teaching hospital where a young man with depression was being evaluated by some of the institution's top practitioners. He asked to be excused to visit the bathroom. When he didn't return they went looking for him and found him hanging by his belt from a pipe. Nobody realized his depression's depth. Shrinks only know what they see, hear and feel. We are not mind readers.

Suicide has been called the ultimate act of rage against the self. It can also be the ultimate act of revenge against loved ones—an everlasting "Screw you." It is especially cruel if the person leaves children.

Suicides essentially take two forms. There's the obvious: a bullet to the brain, hanging oneself or jumping from a tall structure. Then there are the more subtle forms that leave doubt in the minds of those left behind: drug overdoses, slashed wrists and single car auto accidents, for instance. Did they really mean to die, or was it only a cry for help that went bad? Terrible stuff.

Although the act of suicide is selfishness to the extreme, some suicide cases are thoughtful people. I had a great-uncle who did himself in with a shotgun blast to the chest. He pulled the trigger in the middle of the night, waiting until the loud freight train went by, so he wouldn't awaken my grandparents who lived nearby. Everyone agreed what a nice person he had always been so were not surprised by this final considerate gesture. Although this suicide took place about one hundred years ago we family members still occasionally talk about it. It's a glitch in our family's history. Fortunately, the man was a widower with no children.

A colleague had a patient who swallowed enough sleeping pills to put down an elephant, then stepped into an extra large garbage bag and pulled it over her head. She went to sleep but, incredibly, didn't die. "I couldn't even do that right!" she wailed.

"Why the garbage bag?" My colleague asked, not interpreting the obvious symbolism.

"Because I figured I'd lose control of my bowels and urine. I didn't want anyone to have to clean up after me," she said. Very thoughtful.

On the other hand there's the especially mean-spirited suicide. I had a female patient, an accountant for an insurance company. She was twenty-five years old and drop-dead gorgeous. Could have been a movie star. When "Dorothy" was twelve her mother and father divorced. The mother, an alcoholic, ran off with another man. Dorothy remained at home to care for her father. He, too, was an alcoholic. There were no siblings.

Dorothy wanted to be psychoanalyzed because she could not keep a steady boyfriend. She'd been through dozens. She then said, I believe, the dumbest thing I have ever heard from a patient. "I know why I can't keep boyfriends. It's because I'm ugly." She added that she hoped analysis would give her a better personality to make up for her homeliness. "I want to become a more interesting person," she said. At first I thought she was trying to be funny, but she wasn't. She truly thought she was ugly. Unbelievable.

Dorothy was exceptionally talkative and during her first few sessions she rambled on as I listened for the messages between the words—that "third ear" kind of listening. I didn't pick up much except that, obviously, she had a lousy self-image. I also learned she was disgusted by her mother. "She calls me about twice a year. It's always to tell me she has changed boyfriends and she always asks to borrow money. She's never paid me back so I quit sending it to her. She's a loser and a liar."

We were well into her therapy when I asked her about her dad. She had not mentioned him since the first session and we'd been together for many weeks. Mom was a disaster as a mother so I thought perhaps dad was a more positive parental figure. Her eyes welled up, she clasped her hands together on her lap and gazed at the floor. "Too hard," she said, almost inaudibly.

Minutes passed as tears dropped from her eyes onto her dress. She made no attempt to wipe them away. I offered the Kleenex box and she shook her head. It was pure, childlike crying with mucous running from her nose. At last she looked up and took the Kleenex then, half sobbing and half talking told me about her dad.

One evening she and her father had finished supper and Dorothy got up to clear the table, as usual. Her father had been drinking whiskey throughout dinner, as usual. He would then drink himself into a stupor and go to bed without a word to her—his nightly routine. But this night was different. As she was putting the dishes in the sink he asked her to leave the room. She asked why and he said, "For just a minute. I have a surprise." She did as requested and a few seconds later heard a loud "bang" from the kitchen. She ran back to find her father's brains all over the room. She was fifteen years old. That was one mean, rotten way to commit suicide, and that's why his daughter thought she was ugly.

Dorothy and I spent a year together until her career forced her to move away. She was doing okay. Not great, just okay. The image of her dad's brains and blood were still vivid in her memory.

Children of suicides have difficulty experiencing the joy of life, and when they do it is difficult to sustain. Parents who commit suicide cause cancer of the spirit in their children. The only way to cure this cancer is to see a shrink and vent the pent up rage at the deceased parent. They must scream and cry until they are spent ... and then do it again ... and again. In between the screaming and crying they must attempt to understand why their parent committed suicide. In this endeavor the analyst will be invaluable. He will also get them to the point where they know, for sure, it was not their fault, and help them to understand that their parent was most seriously ill, a condition they couldn't possibly have caused. The child of a parent who commits suicide must, eventually, forgive that parent, and here, too, the therapist will be of much value. This could take years, and that's fine, but it must be done. Peace, and a capacity for sustained joy, will come only from understanding and forgiveness.

19

Pissed Off

And Then Some

Surely you know by now many of the maladies that affect our emotional systems are fueled by the amount of anger we have stored in our unconscious minds. This cache of dangerous energy will dictate more than any other factor whether we are at peace with ourselves, and others, or are a bundle of nerves replete with anxiety, fear, guilt, and frustration. It can even dictate our ability, or inability, to love and to be loved, and to experience and sustain joy. Anger is a curse of being human and what is bedeviling is that we can't consciously feel it for what it is. It's just there in the unconscious, eating away at us.

We come by anger naturally and early. At birth we leave our private ocean being pushed and pulled into the harsh world of other people. For the next six months if our needs are not met instantly, we scream bloody murder. As two-year-olds we're frustrated because we can't have and do whatever we want. As four-year-olds we encounter adult logic and reason which makes no sense to us. When six, our eroticized attraction to our parent of the opposite sex is rebuffed.

We are pissed off as teenagers, because we are teenagers, and when adulthood finally arrives we begin to grasp the concept that we are mortal and, someday, will die. The older we get, the more that reality sinks in and it grinds away at us. How many times a day does the thought of dying cross your mind? See what I mean? The inescapability from death is a persistent downer. It's no wonder we are pissed off.

Anger is a form of psychic energy and, like all energy, it cannot be destroyed and must go someplace. Unconscious anger is diverted, disguised and distorted. It messes up the mind and can attack the body as well. Headaches, stomach aches, hypertension, ulcers, and a myriad of other physical problems are often caused by unconscious anger.

Remember, if you don't talk your body will. This is where shrinks come in. There's nothing we can do about eventual death sentences except, perhaps, prolong them. But there's much we can do about the other sources of anger that are inflicting harm on minds and bodies. We crack the door and begin to defuse them.

The confounding thing about unconscious anger is that it is not clean and discernable. When someone wrongs us as an adult it is an immediate source of anger which we can pinpoint and specifically vent. That's easy. Not so with anger which comes from childhood and has been repressed over the years, creating feelings of confusion or malaise instead of outright rage.

You Did What?

Let me tell you about "Brian." In our first session he said he was the son of a converted "love-child" father and sickly mother. Brian referred to this father as a love child because shortly after Brian's mother died, when he was fifteen, his father decided to sleep with every woman in sight, especially young ones. He then shared the stories of his "conquests" with his son. This was in the 1960s when free love, peace, and pot had come into vogue. Before his wife's death Brian's dad was practically Victorian in words and actions. Shortly after the funeral he became an elderly hippy.

Brian had one sibling, a brother four years his senior, who left home after the mother's death and had not been heard from since. Brian remained in the home for two more years until he graduated from high school. Shortly thereafter he received his draft papers from the U.S. Army. At that time the Vietnam War was raging—Brian split.

When Brian first came to see me he was in his late thirties. He'd been married and divorced twice. There'd been no children. In our first session Brian said he had a recurring nightmare. It began when he was a teenager and continued to this day. "At first I'd only have it about once a year. Then it was twice a year, and now it comes about once a month. I heard you could analyze dreams. Do you think you can help? This thing's driving me nuts."

His nightmare was short (most are) and always ended with Brian being strapped into an electric chair. But the people strapping him in were not prison officials, "They were two goons, you know, mafia-guys and I couldn't figure out why I was being put to death instead of them. Just before they'd flip a switch I'd wake up in a sweat. Terrified. My ex-wives said I sometimes screamed." He said when he's awakened by the nightmare his legs are numb and he cannot move them for many minutes.

I told Brian we'd work on the nightmare but first I needed more of his personal history. He agreed to that, telling me, "I've got lots of time and lots of money. You've got to make them go away."

Brian was exceptionally bright with a sophisticated sense of humor. He took to the analytic process as rapidly as anyone I'd ever seen. He knew that his father's sexual behavior was bizarre, even in those liberal times, and that telling him about his lovers was most inappropriate. Brian also knew that his failed marriages, and innumerable other failed relationships, tied directly to his upbringing. Our sessions were lively. He was fun to see. But there was one glaring element. Brian never got upset. No tear showed itself, his chin never quivered, no anger appeared in his eyes. Although he was aware that his past was emotionally disastrous, he consistently found humor in it.

One day I asked Brian what made him angry. After a long pause with uncomfortable body language and a quizzical look he said, " I don't get angry. There is no point to it." I then asked him if he could ever remember being angry at any time in his life. More uncomfortable body language followed—shifting in his chair, crossing and uncrossing his legs and looking out the window. Finally he said, "Well, there was one time I got a little angry, I guess, but mostly I was just doing what I knew I had to do. It's probably not important."

When patients say, "It's probably not important"—it's important. "Let's hear about it," I said and he related the following story.

The day after the Army's draft notice came to his home Brian told his father he was leaving. He said he would contact him from time to time but would not tell him where he was, so his father wouldn't have to lie to the draft board people when they came looking for him.

Brian was a resourceful young man and also had money. During his junior year in high school he decided to deal drugs but distrusted the local sources. During the Christmas holidays he flew to South America to purchase drugs directly. This assured quality control and eliminated middlemen, dramatically increasing his profit margins. He also devised a foolproof way to get his drugs into the United States without being detected. Like I said, he was very bright.

His first stop on his escape from the draft board was Kansas City, where he purchased a new birth certificate and driver's license stating he was twenty-one years of age. He also bought a new social security card and changed his name. From Kansas City he traveled to St. Louis and then worked his way down the Mississippi taking menial jobs. He would work a few weeks, quit, and then stake out his former place of employment for a few days and see if the feds showed up. His father told him they'd been regularly coming to his home. When they didn't show up he knew his new identity was successful. He finally settled in New Orleans and hired on as a stevedore, a very good job for an eighteen-year-old.

Brian was stockily built, about 5 feet, 8 inches tall with a muscular body, so the stevedore job was easy for him and he had no problem doing his share of the work. But soon he encountered a problem with some co-workers. Brian had grown a long ponytail, something dock-workers don't do, and he was soon known as "the hippy." They kept telling him to cut if off. He didn't.

One night after work he went into one of the rough waterfront saloons where his co-workers gathered. They were seated at the bar, and as he walked behind them the biggest and toughest, "Earl," wheeled around on his stool and grabbed Brian's ponytail. With the leverage gained, and surprise, he was able to instantly put Brian on the floor. "Let me buy you a drink you fucking hippy punk," he yelled, and poured his beer into Brian's face. The others surrounded Brian and they, too, poured beer on him. "That ponytail better be gone the next time I see you," Earl threatened as he released his grip. Brian got up and walked out of the bar, derisive laughter following him.

Brian walked down the street and got into his vehicle, an Army surplus truck. (He grinned when he told me this, "Want to psychoanalyze the truck, Jim?") He drove to the telephone booth, looked up Earl's home number, and called it. No answer. "I'd heard his wife left the asshole a couple weeks ago, but I had to be sure." Then he drove to a Kentucky Fried Chicken restaurant, bought a twenty piece bucket, and drove to Earl's trailer, which was in a secluded area of the parish. "He had about five acres of swamp he was proud of," Brian said. "I was there once for a beer blast."

When he got to Earl's place his Doberman charged Brian's truck. Brian opened his window just enough to fit a chicken leg through it. "The fucker tried to bite my finger off," he laughed. "Then he got real interested in the chicken. I opened the window all the way and started throwing pieces of chicken all over the yard and away from the trailer. The dog forgot I was there."

Brian then drove up to the trailer, poured gasoline around it, and gave the area above and under the propane tank an extra dose. He then backed his truck a safe distance away, lit a flare, and threw it against the trailer. In seconds it was engulfed by flames. "One of the prettiest things I've ever seen," Brian laughed. "I was about a half-mile away when the propane exploded. I saw the tank in the rearview mirror. It looked like a huge Roman candle. Fantastic!"

By now I was in shock. "Brian you're putting me on, right?" I said incredulously. "You didn't really burn up the guy's house and kill his dog with chicken bones, did you?"

"No," he said, "The dog didn't die. Dobies are tough to kill." When I regained my composure I asked him what happened when he went to work the next day. (Not an analytic question.)

"I got a lot of weird looks. Everybody thought I did it but they couldn't prove it. Just to be sure I switched tires on the truck. The ones that left tracks at Earl's were floating down the Mississippi. They were half way to the Gulf of Mexico by the time the cops came by. From then on everybody avoided me. I worked on the docks for another year and nobody messed with me or my ponytail again. They figured I was crazy. And I am."

As you can imagine Brian and I spent much time discussing this event in his life. He said he could not recall a feeling of anger toward his attackers. He felt embarrassment while on the floor of the bar but not anger. His decision to "get even" by burning up Earl's house was not spontaneous rage, it took two hours—a calculation. "If I hadn't done something outrageous like that they never would have quit picking on me." He'd reasoned this out before he ever got to his truck.

Up to this time in Brian's analysis he'd spoken almost exclusively about his "hippy father," rarely mentioning his deceased mother. He also entertained me with stories of his felonious life. After the war ended, and the draft board people quit showing up, he quit the stevedore job and returned to the drug business. He was again very successful and expanded his enterprises to include fencing stolen weapons, jewelry and works of art. He made millions but had to be very careful how he spent his money lest the IRS got curious. So he began to acquire small laundromats in cities and towns around the Midwest. "I figured the best place to launder money was in laundromats," he laughed. "It's an all-cash business." By the time he came to see me he owned dozens of them and his life of crime was behind him.

No matter how many stories people have from their pasts they will eventually begin repeating themselves and, after about twenty sessions, this finally happened with Brian. He'd begin a story, realize I'd already heard it, apologize and stop. We then had dead air which was most uncomfortable for him. One day he said, "Well, I guess I've told you just about everything about me. Is it time to terminate?" He knew the lingo.

In the past I had made the mistake of introducing an issue before it was time for the patient to deal with it. But by now I'd been practicing for many years and had learned to keep my mouth shut and let the process evolve on its own. I was most interested in hearing Brian talk about his older brother and, most importantly, about his mother but had bitten my tongue. He now gave me an opening.

"Brian, I've heard lots about your dad and your interesting life since you left home but there's at least two other people in your life that remain a mystery to me."

He laughed and asked, "You mean my brother, the prick, and my mom?"

"Yes."

"I wondered when you were going to ask about them. I'll tell you about my brother first. He's easy. I hate the son-of-a-bitch." Another laugh.

Brian's first memory with his brother was being pinned to the floor. "He held my arms down, sat on my stomach, and let drool from his mouth drop onto my face. If I yelled out some would go in my mouth. It was like torture. I could tell you a hundred stories about that bastard and the shit he did to me." And he did tell me many stories about his brother all ending with, "You see why I hate the son-of-a bitch?"

When the stories wound down a few sessions later, I told Brian I certainly understood why he hated his brother. I asked him why he thought his brother hated him. Brian had never thought that. After a long silence he said, "Isn't it normal for older brothers to pick on younger ones?"

"Not to the degree your brother picked on you," I said, "His actions toward you far exceeded normal sibling rivalry. Something else is going on."

Brian came to his next session leaving his jocular mood behind. "I've been thinking about your question and I think I have the answer. My brother hated me because he blamed me for mom being sick all the time and for her dying young. Could that be it?"

"Maybe so." I said, "Let's hear about mom."

Brian said his mother had been a vibrant, healthy woman until six months after he was born when she contracted multiple sclerosis. Her deterioration was rapid. This realization brought Brian to a remarkable insight: "My brother had a great mom all to himself until I came along. His four-year-old mind would naturally blame mom's illness on my birth which means he blamed me. What else could he think? For the first time in my life I feel sorry for the son-of-a-bitch." He was not laughing. "I'm going to try to find him."

Next Brian and I had to grapple with his relationship with his mother, who eventually became bedridden and unable to do anything for him. Brian said he loved her beyond measure, but his love was unrequited in any tangible way. She was too sick. This, Brian figured out, was the source of his anger. "My emotional mind was built by frustration and unfairness which converted into unconscious rage. Is that right, Jim?"

"Yes, Brian. That's exactly right." He got out of the chair and lay down on the couch.

And, yes, he made the connection of being pinned to the floor by his brother and being pinned to the floor of the bar by his adversaries. "They're lucky I didn't kill them," he laughed, but it was a different kind of laugh. And, yes, he also became aware that he always called his brother "a son-of-a-bitch."

Brian's mother, the bitch (He referred to her as Ma), could not help being sick, but neither could Brian help being angry that he got cheated out of a mom. He loved her and he was furious at her at the same time. Before she was bedridden his mom liked to leave the house to get fresh air and to go to the store. "But she was in a wheelchair and I had to push her. It was embarrassing. I felt like a jerk. Kids teased me about it in school. I hated it! I hated her! It killed me to push her chair but I had no choice." Then he rolled over and covered his face and sobbed, "But I had to do it because I loved her, too!"

Brian had not mentioned his recurring nightmare since our first session. I had tucked it in the back of my mind knowing it would eventually reveal itself. It just did.

I waited for him to stop crying then said, "Brian, we need to talk more about pushing your mom's wheelchair, but first, what comes to mind about being killed by a chair?"

"I don't know what you mean."

"A few moments ago you said it killed you to push her wheelchair."

"I still don't get it."

"What did we talk about in our first session? Why did you come to see me?"

He thought for a few seconds. "Jesus Christ, the electric chair! I always wanted Ma to get an electric wheelchair so I wouldn't have to push her but they were too expensive!"

"Who owned the electric chair in your dream?"

"The mob. No, the Mafia. The MA-fia! Holy shit! That's it!" he said and leapt off the couch.

Brian would never have that nightmare again.

The Mind and I

Early ambivalence is a wrecker ball to the emotions. Brian and I were together for two more years. During that time he found his brother and they are now good friends. He also found "Julie," who is the mother of their three children.

There are many ways of venting anger so it doesn't consume from within. The appropriate way is to talk about it with someone trained to recognize it in its disguised form. Unfortunately most people vent their anger inappropriately by being physically abusive, passively aggressive, grinding their teeth, silently seething, pouting, hurting themselves or getting sick. This isn't good for them or those around them. As far as burning down an adversary's house and attempting to kill his dog, not a good idea. See a shrink instead.

20

Who Saved Your Butt?

Find Out

When listening to my patients tell about their less-than-perfect, sometimes horrific, childhoods I sometimes asked myself, "Who saved their butts?" Yes, they were in analysis and yes, they had a multitude of problems yet they were, in most cases, able to function in their families and in society. They were capable of performing their jobs, loving others and being loved, at least to some degree. It stood to reason that somewhere in their youth or childhood someone must have done something good—to them. Discovering that person, or persons, was an important part of the analysis.

My folks were forty years old when I was born and my sister and brother were seven and eight years older than me. The rule of thumb is: siblings seven or more years older become parental figures in the unconscious minds of their little brothers and sisters. This made me a special case. Instead of two superego figures (parents) I had four of them.

In the 1940s and 50s in my Irish Catholic neighborhood in Chicago there were innumerable rules and regulations, regarding every conceivable thought, word and deed. It was all but impossible to get through a day without committing numerous infractions, most falling into the category of venial sins. "Bad thoughts" were especially numerous and troublesome venial sins and each one carried time in Purgatory. Then there were mortal sins, which could send you to the everlasting fires of hell. Everyone in the neighborhood believed these doctrines, which were reinforced daily by the nuns and priests. Lots of guilt and fear were spawned in that environment. On Saturdays, at Saint Sabina, our parish church, the lines of penitents waiting for Confession were long indeed.

This punitive God lived in my neighborhood but so, too, did the goddamned Devil. We were surrounded. Everyone was fearful of them, including our parents. The underlying emotional atmosphere was tense, due to the heavy blanket of religiosity—absolute Good versus absolute Evil. Living there without guilt was unimaginable. Those weekly Saturday confessions were as much a part of our lives as the attendance at mass on Sunday. I knew no one who did not go to mass every Sunday because to skip it was one of those mortal sins. It was an environment, it seems to me now, that placed more emphasis on not being bad than on being good. I'm getting a headache. (My favorite book, which I read several times in grammar school, was *The Good Bad Boy*. It gave me hope that I was okay and I was appreciative of the guy who wrote it. He obviously was not from the neighborhood.)

Along with these core superego figures in my childhood, others in my life qualified as superego figures albeit to a lesser extent. They were not so vigilant regarding my every thought, word and deed. Nor were they as uptight about God—because they weren't from the neighborhood, either. The first two were my maternal grandparents, "Bapa" and "Granny," who lived on a farm sixty miles from my Chicago home. I spent much time alone with them and, in their eyes, I could do little wrong. I was well into my teens before I abandoned the dream of becoming a farmer, such was their influence on me.

My grandmother continually told me I was a good boy and referred to me as "My Jim." My grandfather, a non-practicing Lutheran, was *laissez faire* with me. We went to town and to the grain elevator in his old Ford. We fed and watered the chickens, gathered the eggs, slopped the hogs, milked the cow and, at haying time, I rode with him on the tractor as he cut and bailed his alfalfa. In his eyes I never screwed up. (He also let me help slaughter the chickens and pluck their feathers, but I don't want to talk about that.)

At home the strongest words I ever heard from the four people superego figures was "shucks" and "doggone it." Down on the farm my grandfather could turn the air blue with his mouth. He also chewed tobacco and smoked cigars. And, get this, my grandmother sometimes said "shit," which she pronounced "shite." God, how I loved those people and they loved me back with nary the raised eyebrow.

It does not make sense that these two non-judgmental people created my mother, who was quite judgmental, but that's the way it was. And this seeming paradox is not unique to my family. We see it all the time; grandparents "saving" their grandchildren who are being constantly scrutinized by their parents—the parents who are the grandparents' offspring. It defies logic and reason. A buddy of mine claims his father was the worst father who ever lived, yet became the best grandfather who ever lived. I knew the man and it was true. Grandparents often save butts.

I got even luckier with butt savers because I also had Aunt Margie and Uncle Bob who lived in Joliet, a small city forty miles from Chicago. In my teens I used to take the train to Joliet and spend weekends with them. They let me stay up watching television until past midnight and fed me exotic dinners such as spaghetti, which my Irish father wouldn't dream of eating. "Too foreign," he'd say. When I got older Uncle Bob, a Lutheran who converted to Catholicism, let me drink a beer and smoke a cigarette, which would be approaching mortal sinfulness at my house. God, how I loved them, too. They accepted me for who I was as I lurched through adolescence. Often aunts and uncles save butts, too.

There is a belief in psychoanalytic circles that the healthiest environment in which to raise children is in the city, not the country. If a kid is stuck on a farm and his parents give him no slack there's not much relief available. It's a numbers game; the more people children are exposed to the better the chances of meeting "butt savers" who validate them as real people. The butcher, the baker, the haberdasher, the cobbler, and the kindly neighbor lady can all help save butts, if only because they know your name and always seem glad to see you. Exposure to people outside of the immediate family is broadening and ego enhancing. The more the merrier, emotionally speaking. Our next door neighbor, Mrs. Stack, had eleven kids. I became her twelfth. She was great. Another of my butt savers. She teasingly called me "Jimmy Jice." I loved it; and her.

You would think a person's butt savers were always known to them. Not so. I always knew I deeply loved my grandparents but until my analysis I was consciously unaware of how very important they were in my emotional development. I learned this about my grandmother, for instance, because of a psychological phenomenon known as a "screen memory." These are memories from our distant past that we recall with clarity. We can bring them into our conscious mind without difficulty and describe them in detail, but they are not literally true. When my analyst asked me what my earliest memory was I had no trouble telling him. I was sitting in the kitchen sink on my grandparents' farm and my grandmother was giving me a bath. I vividly remembered her bathing my back and neck with a wash cloth and how good that felt. I remembered reaching into the soapy water and feeling around for the rubber stopper to let the water out. It was a game we played, "find the stopper." He asked how old I was and I said, "About three."

Screen Memories Are Telling

It didn't take us long to determine this was a screen memory. A three-year-old could not possibly fit in my grandmother's kitchen sink. A six-month-old would have been cramped. So the details of the memory were false but the essence was real. One of the most loving things a parent can do for a kid is give him a gentle bath. So it was my grandmother's overall essence of love for me that the screen memory revealed. I became aware of how truly important she had been to me when I was growing up.

Screen memories are often useful in discovering the opposite of butt savers. They can point out the evil ones. I had a male patient who was certain his first memory was of drinking an entire bottle of lye at his grandmother's house. When I asked him for details he said that when she discovered him writhing in pain on the floor she spanked him.

"How come you didn't die?" I asked. He'd never thought of that and upon further inquiries it turned out his grandmother, who raised him, was the Devil's first cousin. Of course he didn't drink an entire bottle of lye and he may have only touched it. But the screen memory gave us a glimpse of his relationship with his Granny. Among her many faults was being a habitual "liar" (perhaps a clue to the screen memory), and she was also very heavy handed. "She was quick with the switch," he said.

I had a female patient who said her first memory was sitting in her high chair as her mother fed her from her dirty diaper. She clearly remembered the little mound of shit on the spoon coming toward her mouth. That, too, was a screen memory (I think). As the analysis unfolded it became clear my patient's mother was the Devil's sister.

Dreams are similar to screen memories in that the true meaning is hidden behind symbols and they, too, may reveal butt savers. During my analysis I dreamed the following: I was looking at a *Time* magazine cover. On it was Betty Ford, naked, with her legs spread wide apart with knees bent. I was ashamed of myself that I had just dreamed of a former first lady posing like a centerfold. I was embarrassed to tell my analyst.

Of course I did tell him and we began to analyze it. It took the entire fifty minutes but we thought we finally understood it. However, some research on my part was going to be necessary to be certain. The highlights were as follows: "Time" probably meant back in time. Betty Ford's pose could easily symbolize the birthing position. My first association to Betty Ford was that she'd recently had a well-publicized mastectomy. Betty Ford was the first lady—first mother? When Jean asked if anyone close to me had a mastectomy I instantly said, "Aunt Margie."

I made a phone call and learned that when my mom gave birth to me Margie was living with us in Chicago while attending nursing school. She completed her training when I was about nine months old and moved to Joliet to begin her career. With this information we deduced that she was very much like a first mother to me. That explained why I had always felt so very close to her, although I saw her infrequently until my adolescence. It also explained her faith in me as a person even in my hellion days. I wrote her a thank-you letter. Her response discretely validated the meaning of the dream.

I was still living at home in the neighborhood when I graduated from high school. Secretly I now harbored doubts about my Catholic faith. The endless rules seemed trivial, even childish, and the belief that if someone dies in the state of mortal sin he will spend eternity being burned by fire was too cruel and gruesome to believe. Even if God was mean, he couldn't be *that* mean. So my faith was floundering.

My parents insisted I attend a Catholic college (they would be paying for it) so I chose John Carroll University in Cleveland—three hundred miles away. I figured that's where I would slack off practicing my faith. But JCU is taught by Jesuits, an entirely different brand of priests than the ones I'd been exposed to. They are an intellectual order specializing in teaching at the university level. Although devout men, they were also wise to the ways of the world, and there was nothing petty about them. They were adults.

In a freshman theology class I heard, for the first time, that to be a Catholic one must follow the dictates of his *own* conscience. That was good news and it made perfect, adult, sense. Another Jesuit theologian stated that for a person to commit a mortal sin he would really have to work at it. "You would have to consciously and soberly intend to be evil. Few people can do that," he said. Then added, "I never met one." Can you imagine my relief? The Jesuits, too, were my butt savers, religiously speaking. (To change religions from the one you were born into may be an intellectually solid decision, but it can play hell with your emotions.)

It is important for us to discover our butt savers because they reveal truths about us. Knowing, and feeling, as much truth as possible about ourselves is an integral part of the psychotherapeutic process. Butt savers are precious.

21

Ways to Screw Up Kids

Oh So Many

When children are growing up their parents are omnipotent, so it is safe to say they will have an enormous impact on their children's emotional development. Thus when environmentally caused problems arise a parent is at least partially responsible, either directly or indirectly. A direct example of responsibility would be a dad who never hugged or kissed his daughter. It should not be a surprise, then, if she grew up believing she was not all that loveable to men. An indirect example would be a mother who dies in a car accident when her son is six years old. She couldn't prevent the accident but her death will adversely affect his emotional make-up, at least to some degree, for the rest of his life. As a child of my parents, as a parent of four children, after thirty years as a psychoanalyst, and over seventy years as a life observer, I've experienced the power parents have over their offsprings' psyches.

Competing for Their Entire Lives

There are so many ways to screw up kids that dozens of books couldn't hold them all, but here are a few highlights. I have a North-South theory that so upset a man from Boston he grabbed his wife and left a party. The following theory could clear out Fenway Park. It came to me early in my practice and upset me. I tried not to believe it but I saw so much evidence that I know it's true. *Many (perhaps 0smost) parents do not want their children to be better than they are—*

emotionally. In other words, they don't want their kids to be happier than them!

It's fine if the kids have better educations, get better jobs, have bigger houses, and drive more expensive cars. It's not only fine, it's a source of parental pride, "My son the doctor." But if a child is anxiety free, upbeat and loving life, his parents will not be pleased unless they are the same way. If not, they will attempt to bring him back down to their emotional level. The relationship between the parents and their children becomes competitive. If the child winds up in a happier, more compatible marriage than theirs, that will drive them around the bend.

This "don't be happier than I am" syndrome begins when the kids are growing up and acquiring individual personalities, but it's easiest to observe when they become adults. They are free to leave the physical realm of their parents' household, but not their emotional nest. If they do the parents act like they've been slapped. This unfortunate human trait functions, of course, at the unconscious level. Probably no parents alive are consciously aware of not wanting their kids to be happier than they are, but the evidence is pervasive.

"Jack" had passed the Ohio bar exam and was very pleased with himself. He had achieved a major goal and was now armed and ready for adult life. Because he was an exceptionally bright guy he had skated through the academics of college and law school and also had a very good time partying. This partying was a source of constant irritation to his father, who took pride in his own work ethic and sobriety. Jack came home with his good news and called out, "Hey, Dad, I passed the bar!" Without hesitation his father said, "That's the only bar you ever passed." Witty, yes, but it stung Jack and put him back under his father's vigilant scrutiny. The message was clear—don't be so happy and proud of yourself. You're still irresponsible as far as I am concerned. Dad was jealous.

"Ed" brought "Cheryl" home to have dinner with his parents, whose marriage had lost its joy years ago. He'd told his parents earlier that day that she was the girl of his dreams and he hoped to marry her. At dinner Ed's mom asked Cheryl where they'd met. Cheryl said that she and her friends had been to rock concert and were standing next to Ed and his friends. "Oh," said Ed's mother, "so you were a pick-up?" (Ed, by the way, had already told his mother where they'd met, so she had time to practice her nasty comment.)

Ed and Cheryl did marry but as you can imagine the relationship between Ed's mother and wife was strained. This was a constant irritant for Ed and he dreaded the times the two women in his life were together. His mother would not let up. Once when visiting she said, "Cheryl, let me fix breakfast. I know exactly how my Eddie likes his eggs," implying that Cheryl didn't. Ed, of course, should have told his mother to butt out but he wouldn't or couldn't, which pissed off Cheryl. Mom, meanwhile, was having a grand time keeping her Eddie and his marriage off balance, unconsciously wishing it would deteriorate like her own.

A psychoanalytic adage states the best way to treat kids is with "benign neglect." This is debatable when kids are little but it certainly is true when they've left home. Don't call them. Let them call you.

The Mixed Message

The mixed message is an eye-crosser which probably does more damage than any other factor in raising kids. Jealousy toward one's children is a classic mixed message. The parents say they want only the best for their children yet the kids feel the jealousy when they marry soul mates and lead lives that are relatively stress free. It will be no time at all before their parents are complaining about their own lives and marriages, thus throwing cold water on their children's happiness.

Telling your kids you are going to do something and then doing the opposite is a mixed message. "Tomorrow we're going to the zoo. Won't that be fun?" But when tomorrow comes there's too much work to be done around the house. "But we'll go sometime soon." Set 'em up—knock 'em down.

"Daddy loves you so much, you're the most important person in the world to me." says daddy. But the little girl thinks, "But Daddy works all the time and I rarely see him and, besides, isn't Mommy supposed to be the most important person in the world to him?" (As a wise person once said, "The most important thing a man can do for his children is to love their mother.")

The Mind and I

No child of any age can fathom the following: "Mommy says she loves me, and daddy says he loves me but they no longer love each other and are getting divorced. They used to love each other, what happened? What have I done wrong?" Want to screw up your kids? Get divorced. It's a high powered mixed message with unending fallout.

If you are a sober, responsible and loving person during the day and a staggering, speech slurring, abusive drunk at night you are a walking mixed message unto yourself and to your children.

Following is a litany of things not to say: A divorced mother to her child, "Of course it's okay for you to visit your father. I just hate every minute you are not with me. All I do is cry till you come back. Now go and have fun." (Sure, kid, try to have fun while mommy's home crying.)

"No one will ever love you as much as I do." (You're screwed, kid.)

The child has been told often that cheating and lying are bad. Once I heard an acquaintance answer a waitress's question, as she pointed to her child, "How old is your daughter?" The kid, I knew, was seven. The mother answered, "six," so her child's breakfast would be free. (You should have seen the little girl's face.)

A parent says to his twenty-something son, "I enjoyed talking to your girlfriend, she seems like a nice person, but did she go to college?" (Zap.)

"I want only what's best for you, and nobody knows what's best for you better than me," says dad. (Uh, oh," thinks the kid.)

"You can accomplish whatever you put your mind to." (Excuse me?)

"You can be whoever you want to be, just don't ever forget where you came from." (Huh?)

Tell a kid to do something, notice that he didn't so it, and let it pass. Or tell a kid not to do something, watch him do it, and say nothing. Mixed messages not only cross eyes, they confuse little minds. "What am I supposed to do, or not do, really?" they ask. "Who is the boss around here anyway? Not me, I hope, I'm too young." Mixed messages are terribly harmful.

When I was a kid I had an annual mixed message every fall when visiting my grandparents' farm. My grandfather took particular pride in his chickens. He had the healthiest, best looking flock for miles around. Everybody said, "Ed Wurtz sure loves his chickens." Yet every autumn I watched him catch his chickens, chop their heads off on a wooden block, dip their carcasses in boiling water and pluck their feathers. I loved my grandfather but was understandably ambivalent about wanting him to love me.

Encouraging Oedipus

When kids are around four or five years old, and again around puberty, you will recall they are especially attracted to their parents of the opposite sex. The wise parents gently, but firmly, rebuff the child's overtures so he or she will emulate and identify with the parent of the same sex.

But many parents are not wise and instead of gently rebuffing they encourage this newfound, semi-erotic, attention. A colleague had a patient who, when she was a little girl, told her daddy she wanted to marry him when she grew up. This was a perfectly normal, rational statement for a seven-year-old to make. But the father, instead of saying something like, "That makes me happy, Honey, but I'm already married to mommy," went out and bought his daughter an engagement ring. She delightedly wore the ring for months until one day she overheard her father laughing about it to friends. Twenty years later she still recalled her pain and shame.

I had a patient whose divorced mother began inspecting his penis at age four, "Just to make sure it's growing." She continued to do this until her son was twelve, when he finally got up the courage to tell her to stop. He grappled with his sexuality, and his anger toward mom in particular and, women in general, for many years.

You'd be surprised how many parents sleep in the same bed with their children of the opposite sex claiming nothing sexual ever takes place. Even if this is true, and I believe it is in most cases, its still a bad idea. It's an inappropriate setting, encouraging the erotic Oedipal attraction.

This hardly needs to be said, but it's so important that it cannot be emphasized enough. If you really want to mess with your kid's mind and leave an emotional wound that will never heal, act out with that child sexually. This is not only a mixed message that will destroy a spirit, it is mortal sin. Incest is frighteningly common (in all economic brackets) between father and daughter and older brother with younger sister. So, too, is implied incestual desires from mothers to their sons, although it is rare that they go "all the way."

There are lots of other ways to screw up the Oedipal phase besides engagement rings, penis checking and acting upon your child's (and your) sexual attraction. Allowing your kid of the opposite sex to see you naked, if only briefly, is seductive and inappropriate and should be avoided. A two-second glimpse of a parent's crotch, breasts, buttocks or penis is a mind photo that will last a lifetime.

On the flip side of the Oedipal conflict are those parents who react harshly to the overtures of their children of the opposite sex. Fathers are the main culprits here. They get distant with their daughters or they bark at them. When the second Oedipal phase comes along at puberty, frightened by his feelings, a father may make statements like, "Women are air-heads," or other words denigrating their daughter's gender. They may criticize their daughter's dress, call her a slut, make fun of her looks, and belittle her friends. Sometimes they get heavy handed with their daughters, which is a counterphobic display of their real feelings. Mothers usually do better with the flip side of Oedipus. They do not have to "push" their boys away as much as fathers do their daughters.

How parents handle the Oedipal Conflict will affect their children for the rest of their lives, just like the other stages of psychological development. But Oedipus is key in preparing children for the ultimate and most important adult relationship—marriage. Again, the key guideline is to gently but firmly push the child toward the parent of the same sex. Easy to say, not so easy to do. Gently but firmly. Almost a paradox.

Of course the question is now begged: "What about in cases of death or divorce, where there's only one parent in the home?" This is indeed a problem. Call in the grandparents, aunts and uncles, friends, neighbors, teachers and preachers who can pinch-hit as adult role models. They will help to lessen the mess the death or divorce has created in a child's emotional system. But lessen is all they can do.

When parents get divorced they should never denigrate an ex-spouse in front of the children. Trashing their mother or father is a terrible thing to do to kids. When they become adults the kids can figure out themselves what went wrong with the marriage, if they choose to do so. Meanwhile, bite your tongue. (Good luck.)

Let's Be Friends

Another surefire way to confuse a kid is to become his "buddy." Kids cannot empathize with or understand the experience level of their parents. For parents to regress to the child's level is suspicious (what is their emotional age?) and unfair to the child. Kids need their folks to be firmly established as adult role models into which they can grow.

Parents cannot be friends with their kids until they are grown up and permanently gone from the nest. Even then, it's an iffy proposition. Kids and parents of all ages should have their own friends. That's the best way to grow and continue to grow.

A classic culprit is the Little League dad who gets upset at his son, the umpires, and the coaches. When things aren't going as he wishes, he begins yelling and generally making an ass of himself. He becomes one more ten-year-old and is an embarrassment to his child. Parents at Little League games should be there for one reason—to cheer.

I have had women patients whose mothers made them into friends at an early age. Their mothers' idea of friendship was having a person they could tell their troubles to. Can you imagine a mother complaining about her lot in life to her six-year-old daughter? Happens all the time, much to the daughter's detriment. One of my patients, by the time she entered puberty, had gone beyond being mom's friend. She had become mom's mom. The child assumed the role of parent to the emotionally infantile mother thus was cheated out of having a parent herself. She had no one to turn to in her times of crisis or stress. She not only had to mother her mother she also had to mother herself.

I had a male patient who grew up in the sixties in what was supposed to a psychologically enlightened family. There was no discipline and from his earliest years he was treated as an equal by his parents. He was told to address them by their first names. During his high school years he "acted out" with truancies, lousy grades, and scrapes with the law regarding alcohol and drugs. He got a classmate pregnant. Whenever his parents learned of these transgressions they simply cried. My patient became a sociopath in adulthood. He had nothing but scorn for society, which, to him, was merely a replacement of his flawed parents.

Kids need to be with other kids. Receiving verbal abuse, getting feelings hurt, being chastised and teased is best when it comes from other kids. So, too, is being praised. Peers are great preparers for adult life.

You're My Favorite

If there is more than one child in the family parents should never tell one of them that he or she is their favorite. This is a cruel thing to do to that kid. His sibling(s) will resent him and the pressures to continue to be favorite takes a toll. One of my male patients was frequently told by his mother that he was her favorite, but that it was a secret and made him promise not to tell the others. Of course he did tell—how could he not—he was a kid. When they became adults he was the one who needed therapy. His siblings were fine. In reality, parents might have a favorite child, probably the one who's least like them. They must keep this information to themselves.

Pets

One of my patients, "Marie," was a forty-two-year-old attorney. Her parents had tried for years to have a child without success and eventually decided to adopt. Marie was three days old when they brought her home. During the many years of childlessness the parents raised Yorkshire terriers as a hobby, showing them at AKC functions around the South. The bitch that won the most prizes was named "Honey." Marie told me that she hated Honey because Honey got ten times more attention than she did. "You should have seen how they fawned over her—grooming, bathing, petting, kissing. Hell they never even touched me."

Coincidentally (I'm sure) I had another attorney patient named

"Dan." Dan described his father as being very harsh with him over the least infraction and often took off his belt and wailed away at Dan and his two brothers. "He was the most unbending, unloving bastard who ever lived," Dan said.

I asked him if his father ever showed kindness. "Yes," he said, "but only to his dog. The goddamned thing could shit in the middle of the kitchen floor and my father thought it was funny. My brothers and I would have to clean it up, of course. I hated that fucking mutt."

If there are pets in the house when children are growing up those pets should belong to the children, not the parents. Sibling rivalries cause enough frustration; a kid should not have to compete with an animal for the parents' love and attention.

Sticks and Stones

Can break my bones but words will never hurt me. This saying could take top prize for being the dumbest of all. Following are some statements that were made to my patients by their parents:

> I wish you were never born.
> You will never amount to anything.
> You are a slut.
> Why can't you be like your brother (sister)?
> I really don't know where you came from.
> You're a loser.
> You have a terrible personality.
> You'll be miserable all your life.
> There's nothing lovable about you.
> You're the most selfish person I know.

The emotional mind is programmed by statements like these, which leave an indelible mark. Words cannot only hurt children, they can kill them ... emotionally.

All therapists have had the following experience. The phone rings and it is a parent, usually a mother, who wants to make an appointment for her child. The therapist wisely says, "Okay, but why don't you come in first and tell me about your child. Then we'll see how to proceed."

The mom shows up, talks for perhaps three minutes about her kid, then inevitably segues the conversation onto herself and her problems. Months later she will still be talking about herself, never mentioning her child. This is how it should be. Few kids need psychotherapy. If a child is screwed up, his or her parents should seek help to gain insight into their own problems. They'll then discover what is really going on with their kid.

Compliments with Caveats

This syndrome is so common (and subtle) it is often missed in analysis yet it can break spirits and cause lifelong malaise. Give kids compliments but never purely, always attaching a barb, a yes but, and almost, a too bad, a tsk, a tat, a caveat. For instance:

- That was a nice catch you made, Jimmy, saving a home run, it's too bad you later struck out.
- Honey, you look beautiful in that new dress, if you lost some pounds we could send you to Hollywood.
- This is a pretty good report card, Andy, four A's but the one B spoiled it.
- You did a wonderful job cleaning your room, Zack, but the bedspread is crooked.
- Congratulations, Walt, on breaking the scoring record but don't let it go to your head because your teammates deserve most of the credit.

You get the point. Taken alone none of these tweaks is a big deal but hundreds or thousands of them heard over many years sends a powerful message: Kid, you're not quite right.

Parents, get your heads out. Either compliment or correct but not at the same time and, for heaven's sake, not in the same sentence!

22

They're Just Babies, Too, You Know

Fragility Is Ours

The theme throughout this book has been: when a person is emotionally messed-up he or she was made that way, in most instances, from childhood experiences. This is not my idea, I've just brought it to your attention. Everybody in the mental health field encounters this truth every day.

Kids are helpless. Whatever they receive they get from adults including food, clothing, shelter and neuroses. After five years of full-time practice I began to hate this truth. It was anguishing hearing stories all day, every day, of what people had done to their children. It also began to erode my faith in the essential goodness of my fellow man. I began playing a secret game as I listened to my patients' histories. I called it, "Where's the free will?" As they told of their life choices—marital partners, careers and life styles I would ask myself, "How much did the emotions play, versus the intellect, in making those choices?"

I had a patient, "Sherry," who had chosen a dimwit, "Harry," to be her loving, wedded husband. Prior to the marriage Harry already drank too much, lived with his parents, couldn't keep a steady job, sold dope on the side, had a mean streak and showed her little kindness. But she said, in his (and her) defense, that he was very handsome, was great in bed, and loved his dog. They'd been married less than a year. He was cheating on her, drinking more than ever, had quit work completely and, two weeks prior to her appointment, he beat her up when she threatened to leave him. Now she was afraid to leave, having no place to go. I determined that in picking Harry, Sherry's emotions bested her intellect by a score of one hundred to zero. Her choice was based on rushes, gushes, wishes, and hopes. She didn't have one brain cell working to aid her in seeing that Harry was a user and a loser. And now the bastard was beating her up. While sitting on my leather chair, feet on the ottoman, I decided that human beings have scant amounts of free will. Hell, sometimes I couldn't find any! Emotions ruled the roost.

I'd silently seethe at Sherry's parents and all my patients' parents, and everybody else's parents going all the way back to the nincompoops, Adam and Eve—who screwed everything up to begin with—precipitating the need for all the Sherrys, Marys and Larrys to come sit in my winged-back chair or lie on my couch. Sherry was programmed to be romantically attracted to the likes of a Harry and there was nothing she could do about it. I became jaded and cynical. I began to take personally the unfairnesses heaped on my patients and became angry at the unfairness of their lives. The phone rang at all hours and off I'd dash to mend another mind. Meanwhile (the evidence is there), my mind was beginning to slip. I developed this recurring fantasy that there was only so much mental health to be had in my consultation room and as my patients got better, I got worse.

"I'm seeing ten patients a day and they are sucking my bone marrow," I said one day to a colleague. "You better take a vacation," he replied.

One night my doorbell rang at 1 a.m. It was one of my patients. He was drunk. "I just thought you might want to know that I'm going over to that bitch's apartment (his estranged wife) and kill her and her boyfriend. I have a gun."

"Come on in and let's talk about it first," I said. (Shit!)

Of course I knew he wanted me to talk him out of it, why else would he be here? But this took over two hours as he sobered up, finally listened to reason and gave me the gun. It was loaded.

When practicing in a small town it is impossible to see only those patients who are capable of psychoanalysis. Not only is the cost prohibitive, because it takes years, but also many people simply do not have the capacity for insight which is necessary for that mode of therapy. But I had to make a living so I took what came in the door and much of that was crisis intervention: the suicidal, the histrionic, the first time offenders appointed by the court, the "acting outers" and marriage problems. Practicing in depth psychoanalysis is pure joy, but crisis intervention is a pain in the ass, at least it was for me. (Some psychotherapists, God bless them, thrive on it.)

I desperately did need a vacation, a long one, but I couldn't take it because I'd come to believe my patients desperately needed me. I had regressed from being a psychoanalyst to being a savior. Perspective is a gift and I'd lost it. The forest disappeared and the trees overwhelmed. I quit.

Of course I didn't really quit. That would be an abandonment of my patients, which truly would have harmed some of them. But I did quit taking new patients and two years later I was a full-time businessman and part-time shrink. I'd regained my perspective by cutting back on my practice and was able to cope with the unfairness of "people making" because I was exposed to it in smaller doses. Good for me. Good for my patients.

To be candid, it was also nice to again make money I could depend on. When I began backing down from full-time practice the economy was in shambles, interest rates were at record highs and many of my patients were struggling to make ends meet. So "Dr. Savior" carried them to my own detriment. One, a realtor, took six years to finally clear up his bill. But, again, that's enough about me. Let's get back to parents.

Revenge

Parents can continue to adversely affect their children's lives, even when they've become adults, by discouraging them from seeking psychotherapy. Most parents think when their past behavior is scrutinized their images in their children's minds will be radically altered. Therapy, therefore, is threatening to them.

What they don't realize is that when therapy is conducted properly over a lengthy period of time, their relationship with their children will improve; it certainly won't get worse, even though much will be discovered regarding the parents' past mistakes. And, yes, with the encouragement of the therapist parents will, for a time, be verbally crucified by their children for their ineptness—but not to their faces, only in the therapist's office. Redemption will then follow as the patients begin to understand that their parents are simply human beings, full of flaws like all human beings, and in most cases they will see they did the best they knew how. They did to their kid, without malice, that which was done to them. I am unaware of any permanent rifts, and very few temporary ones, between patients and their parents because of psychotherapy. One of its goals is to understand and forgive. That's not the stuff of rifts. It's the stuff of healing.

What patients eventually learn about their parents is that the treatment they received from them was administered *unconsciously*. They will also learn to remove their parents from the unrealistic pedestal of power that every child erects. It was supposed to be there in childhood but not any more. They'll learn that their parents are limited in their capacity to love and they are psychologically naive. They'll learn their parents are simply people, you know, dunderheads. And most importantly they'll learn in therapy that almost everyone is a psychoanalytic dunderhead—it's a matter of degrees and it's time to give parents some slack.

Parents cannot possibly control all of the psychological influences that relentlessly bombard their children. Even if the mother stays home until the kids go to school (which is the ideal), she can't protect them from negative influences from neighbors, relatives and other kids. If she must return to work after her baby is born there is no way she can really know how her infants and toddlers are being treated by the babysitters and the day care centers.

When the kids start school they'll be exposed to dozens of peers and, of course, teachers who become parental figures. There will also be clergy, scout leaders, coaches and other kids' parents who will also affect, for better or worse, the children's impressionable, developing minds. Television and the Internet will also be customizing influences on their unconscious. Even the most vigilant parents can't monitor every remote button pushed or icon clicked. Parents can only control their own actions, or non-actions, words or silences, regarding their children's emotional well-being. When "Life" enters the equation of child-rearing, parents (even the atheists) do a hell-of-a-lot of praying.

There are "adult children" who truly resent their parents for their previous transgressions, slights, mistakes and absenteeism. Today their parents are getting up in years and their adult children have learned what buttons to push to make these parents feel guilty. They harangue them endlessly and feel justified in doing so. To those parents I offer the following advice:

1. Listen to all of your adult child's complaints. If you think they have a point (and they probably do) sincerely apologize.
2. Repeat number one above about three more times.
3. If that doesn't silence them, and in most cases it won't, suggest that they seek psychotherapy. If you are able, offer to pay for a portion of it—but only a portion. They must contribute or they won't be totally forthcoming to the therapist.
4. If they refuse to listen to this suggestion—then you've got trouble. They are going to spend the rest of your life berating you. Their wounds are deep and they want revenge. Return to number one above, one more time, adding these words at the end: "I did the best I could, all things considered. Now kindly leave me alone. I don't deserve this." And you probably don't. But even if you do, there's not a damned thing you can do about it now.

In psychotherapy we learn that we are all childlike, emotionally. For instance, there is a huge intellectual difference between the little boy in first grade and the nuclear physicist he becomes. Not so much so emotionally. What hurt his feelings at age six will likely hurt them at fifty-six.

One of the wisest things I ever heard about this reality was said by Barbara. Her parents had experienced much of life and had traveled the world. Her dad was a Ph.D. and a scholar. Her mom had a master's degree and a successful career. He had flown B-29 bombers during World War II. Her mother had grown up on the edge of the Everglades—alligators and poisonous snakes were frequent visitors to her back yard. Life had often tested their mettle but they always persevered, overcoming whatever obstacles were placed in their paths. These were people of substance.

The Mind and I

Shortly after Barbara and I were married her parents planed to visit. I told her I had a tennis game scheduled for the night they were arriving so I wouldn't be there to greet them. She looked at me with her new-wife eyes and said, "They're just babies, too, you know." The dunderhead psychoanalyst cancelled the tennis game.

23

Should I See a Shrink?

Why Do You Ask?

My buddy, "Ralph," teaches at a major university. He is about as bright a guy as I've ever met and one of the most well rounded. He can expound on any topic from the physical sciences, the formation of black holes, Shakespeare, classical music, the stock market, the Greeks, you name it. One night at the school's annual fund raising gala he and I were discussing a mutual friend, "Edward," who was coming unglued. Edward was a mathematical genius and a tenured professor at the university. We learned that in the middle of class he tipped over his desk, told his students they were a bunch of fucking morons; told his boss the same thing and resigned. Soon his wife left him and took the kids. He was in his house, alone, drinking day and night.

"How would you diagnose him?" asked Ralph.

"I don't know," I said. "Depression, mania, perhaps some phobia got loose and overwhelmed him. It doesn't matter."

"How can he be treated without a diagnosis?" Ralph asked.

"Easy. Get him dried out, evened out, and then ask him to tell you about himself."

"Of course," he said, mock hitting his forehead with the heel of his hand.

Even the brightest often forget. It's too simple and doesn't seem right. Mental illness should be much more complicated than that but, bafflingly, it usually isn't.

Once Edward told me, "My life is a losing battle. I see no hope." He was a man with a wonderful wife, kids and nice house. He was published and respected by his peers. With his professorship came prestige. The life battle he was losing was, obviously, within his mind. I suggested that he seek psychotherapy and volunteered to recommend someone. I could not see him because we were friends. "Psychoanalysis is a bunch of bullshit," he angrily said, "all that Oedipal Freud crap about me wanting to sleep with my mother."

Perhaps I should have been insulted, he just called my profession bullshit, but he was in such an agitated state I wasn't even mildly offended. In fact, I laughed out loud. What I could have said, but didn't, was that there was a flip side to Oedipus. His mother also wanted to sleep with him, but I thought I'd leave that startling piece of news to his therapist, if he ever found one.

Once a professional athlete, after learning I was a psychoanalyst, said, "I went through therapy for about a year. I really enjoyed it and learned a lot." Naturally I was pleased to hear this and told him so. Then he added, "We talked about things no one will ever know about." Naturally I did not add, "You want to bet?"

All patients in therapy talked about the same "things," and there aren't that many of them. They think their experiences are unique, and they are, but only in the details. The dynamics in the unconscious are the same with everyone. The reason Edward the professor flipped over his desk, denigrated his students and boss, resigned and alienated his wife and kids was simple. The man was full of rage, which was manufactured at an early age. Finding the sources of his rage would not be difficult, but getting him to relive the manufacturing process, both intellectually and emotionally, then re-direct the rage and eventually diffuse it would not be simple. It could take years.

The problem is our defense mechanisms. They are elusive, multi-layered, strong as granite, and slippery as wet clay. Each layer of defense must be discovered, examined, understood and re-felt. This layer must be slowly removed before the next layer is tackled. Psychoanalysis has been compared to peeling an onion. We analysts are cautioned not to hurry this process (as in slicing the onion) because each layer has its own important reason for being. With particularly ill patients if we go too fast and arrive at the raging fire of anger too soon, we will allow in too much oxygen (truth). Then we really have a mess on our hands. The fire will burn up the already fragile ego (person). It took decades for patients to get to the crisis point in their lives. To think they can be fixed rapidly with counseling and few interpretations is not only dangerous, it is dumb.

This is not to say that counseling and some well-chosen words do not have their place. Often that's all that is needed to get someone back up and running. School counselors and clergy come to mind as well as wise parents and good friends. But if you think talking to the desk flipper will make him better, don't aspire to be a psychotherapist. He's the one that's got to do the talking. But, by now, you know that. (Note: Edward did not seek help. A year or so later this brilliant man killed himself.)

I have often been asked if everyone should to go through psychotherapy. The answer is "no." Some people are genuinely happy, loving and most comfortable in their own skins. And, equally important, their families and friends find them delightful to be with. They do not need psychotherapy.

Those who do need therapy are among the following: suicidal; unreasonably fearful; frequently stymied by guilt. Any emotional state where a feeling of well-being is unattainable or unsustainable, without apparent reason, qualifies as a need for therapy. Also, those who cannot make and maintain friendships over an extended period would benefit from therapy. Certainly people who can't stay married, or are miserable in that state, should see a shrink. The two common complaints I heard most often from new patients were: (1) I'm thirty-five years old. My life is half over. If the next half is as empty as the first half what's the point? (2) I know a hundred people who are married but none that are happy. And my marriage, for sure, sucks. (Time for the "T" sign.)

One of the confounding things about many people is that it is easy for them to love, but almost impossible for them to *be loved*. That's often a marriage tilt. When we are doing the loving we are in control. As recipients of love we are vulnerable. Being vulnerable is too scary for many. In his famous prayer St. Francis of Assisi, stated: "For it is in loving that we are loved. It is in giving that we receive." That's true, Francis, but it's not the whole story. In receiving love we also give. We give our trust, which is a great gift. Therapy teaches trust.

You'll Enjoy Yourself

I have written about pain and tears in the analytic process, and they are part of it, but mostly it is fun. Getting to talk about yourself without interruption and learning truths about you (the "Holy cows!" and "That's rights!") are a pleasure to experience for both analyst and analysand. The usual mood in a shrink's office is not a somber one. Rather it is upbeat about the good things happening and hopeful for better things to come.

It is understandable that fear and trepidation accompany the first visit to a shrink (it certainly was for me), but soon those visits will be the highlight of a patient's week. What could be more valuable or more interesting than learning more and more about oneself? And this learning process, actually a growth process, doesn't end when the therapy ends—it will continue for the rest of life. I know it sounds like I'm "selling" and I am. But I'm doing it for you, not for me. I'm retired.

And It Makes Sense

By now, you have a pretty good idea of what it's like to be a patient and also a shrink. You've learned some basic theories on the working of the emotional system. You have been exposed to the unconscious mind and its powers. The concept of psychotherapy is no longer mysterious.

You've learned the unconscious mind does not follow the rules of logic, reason and common sense. Its prime intent is to perpetuate itself without change—like the broken record—repeating the same dynamics over and over and over again with no concern whether the outcome is good or bad. If the outcome is invariably bad the unconscious mind could not care less. That doesn't make sense.

It is a paradox, then, that it is precisely common sense that can correct a faulty unconscious. For instance, if a woman continually finds herself in abusive relationships she should learn why. To do this we go back in time to discover when this pattern began, and who caused it.

This is done by remembering and feeling events from the past and talking about them, thus taking these causes (the people) out of the unconscious mind and into the open. They are defined, understood and put into perspective. Now she can deal with them. She has exposed them to the bright lights of the analytic process so they can no longer lurk in the dark waiting to pounce. They (the people) have been "found out." This is eminently sensible.

It is not logical or reasonable to accomplish something wonderful and then screw it up. It is stupid to hit a crushing line drive into right-center field and then lollygag around the bases only to be thrown out at home plate. It is even dumber to get a promotion at work then later at the office Christmas party, with a snoot full of booze, tell your boss that at times he can be a real asshole. It is ludicrous to marry the girl of your dreams and one year later begin taking her for granted causing her to resent you. None of these actions make sense.

But to go back in time and discover that these are not isolated instances but patterns of self-destructive behavior which can be traced to the present—that does makes sense.

The Naysayers Will Always Be With Us

Psychotherapy is offensive to many people for many reasons. To begin with we therapists assume that everyone, our patients and ourselves, have some mighty nasty things going on in our minds. Things we'd rather not own up to. Things that are considered sinful. Feeling great fury at a deceased parent, for instance, is not something most people would admit to. Admitting to certain sexual fantasies; feeling secretly gleeful when a friend falls on hard times; being distraught when a sibling is doing better than we are; secretly thinking it would be neat if the boss got sick so we could have his job; feeling smug when our kid makes the team and our neighbor's kid doesn't, etc. These are all thoughts that most would agree are unkind. I agree, too, but I also know they are within us, whether we admit to them or not. The essence of psychoanalysis, psychotherapy, "the talking cure" or whatever you want to call it, is to get patients to be honest about their emotions. This can be difficult and at first glance appear to be in conflict with our society, which encourages us to deny or instantly repress "evil" thoughts. It takes guts to do just the opposite—admit to them, get them out in the open, and expunge them.

But if we do this we'll, paradoxically, become better people. Our base wishes, fears, and guilts (that everyone shares) will be exposed and released into consciousness where they can be laughed at and discarded. By taking the lid off of our "evilness" we've defused it. In other words, "The growth of the ego weakens the id."

So it's okay to wish that our pompous neighbor falls off his ladder, but we can't pull it out from under him. Or to fantasize an ex-spouse runs into one of those blow-em-up trucks. Evil thoughts aren't evil, only evil actions are.

The study of the emotional system has taught us over the last hundred years there are unkind, jealous, selfish, petty, mean-spirited sides to every human mind. These unholy thoughts and feelings lurk in the unconscious, occasionally popping to the surface and showing themselves—often to the horror of their owners. ("I didn't mean that!") Then they slip back into the dark. When people deny possessing these negative thoughts and impulses they set themselves up for emotional problems.

Also stashed in the unconscious are repressed (forgotten) memories of our imperfect childhoods. Children are sometimes physically and sexually abused—either directly or by innuendo. They may also be emotionally (or literally) abandoned, ignored, lied to, put down, made to feel frightened or insecure, pushed beyond their limits, slighted and ridiculed. No kid is immune from at least some of these elements of childhood. If severe enough and left festering and unexamined, they, too, can lead to mental illness. Painful memories need to be exorcized into consciousness where they can be dealt with. If properly done, such exploration can't hurt. It can only make people better. Getting at, and properly dealing with, unconscious feelings and memories can-not be done alone, however. Only with the assistance of another per-son can this be accomplished. Our repressed feelings and memories are so intertwined, compressed, and disguised we cannot untangle them alone.

184

Therapy Shopping

Unfortunately, friends or family members won't be of much help. First of all, they don't know what to listen for. Secondly, they'll have preconceived notions about us (and maybe an ax or two to grind) and we'll never be able to trust them to the point of complete candor. They're not neutral. They'll be judgmental. They can't help it. So we must find a professional psychotherapist if we're to delve into our unconscious.

How does one find a therapist? They are all over the place so finding them is easy. Finding a good one may not be so easy, however, because the mental health field attracts many emotionally flaky people. Before committing to a specific therapist ask the following:

- Has therapist been in therapy prior to going into practice? If not, keep looking.
- Does he or she have at least five years of experience?
- Does therapist consider himself to be analytic or more "direct counseling?" If the latter, he will not be treating your unconscious mind. Leave.
- Will you be considered patient or client? If client, same as above.
- What is his fee? If it isn't at least $150 per hour (2014 prices) he's insecure; keep looking. (If it is $150 or more, and that's too much for you, ask if he'll consider less. He probably will.)
- Is the therapy offered faith-based? If so, walk away. There is nothing wrong with counseling with a religious bent for spiritual growth and enlightenment, but that is not psychotherapy. Faith-based counseling is not designed, or equipped, to probe the unconscious mind.
- Lastly, if the therapist suggests a written contract outlining frequency of treatments, duration of the therapy, and numerous do's and don'ts, tell him you feel that is contrived. Walk out. You are about to explore your unconscious and there's no predicting where the process will lead or how long it will take.

Psychoanalysis is designed to do the following:

- End depression and anxiety.
- Eliminate or greatly abate neuroses, which include phobias.
- Put an end to physical symptoms which are psychosomatic.
- Enhance one's abilities to love, be loved, work and create.

These are realistic, legitimate expectations from the process. Because analysis deals with the dynamics of the unconscious mind (that combative relationship between id and superego), it transcends cultures and societies. The id is below them and predates them. It comes first. The id says, "Gimme, gimme, gimme." When the superego says, "No you can't do (have, wish for, feel) that," the ego then must arrive at a compromise. That's the way *everybody's* mind works. Acquiring this realization is broadening and makes life more understandable and fun. Now when we hear the movie actor described as "mysterious, complicated and moody," we are no longer intrigued. We'll know the truth. He has emotional problems. Healthy people aren't moody. They are upbeat and predictable.

Another positive result that comes from being analyzed is that the discipline makes people more tolerant of others because they have become aware that:

1. In any conflict they may be the one who is at fault, so before they become defensive, or lash out, they'll give their personal history of their feelings some thought regarding the dynamics of that conflict.
2. Because they know everyone has unconscious forces working within, they will be prone to be more forgiving. Their understanding of others has been heightened, so they become more tolerant, nicer people.

Being analyzed makes it easier to comprehend the actions of some of history's more vicious characters, Hitler, for instance, because we know that this deranged mass murderer was taking out displaced rage on fellow human beings as revenge for his terrible childhood. Remember there is no connection between the emotions and intellect; thus this awful human being was shrewd enough and bright enough to get into a position of power. Then he could do unto others what was done unto him—millions of times over.

Being analyzed also makes it easier to comprehend the terrible events that constantly bombard us from the media. Some years ago a young mother murdered her two children. She drowned them because her new boyfriend didn't like kids. "How could she so it?" was the question asked by everyone who followed this awful story. She must have gone crazy; she's just plain evil; she must have been possessed by the Devil; these were some of the reasons given. But these words are nebulous. Her unspeakable crime demands answers that are more sensible. Those who've been analyzed are attuned to psychic determinism and realize that positive input during childhood creates emotional assets, while negative ones create liabilities.

From news reports we got a glimpse of the psychic determinism that molded the mother's emotional balance sheet. When she was eight years old her father blew his brains out. When he pulled the trigger, he emotionally bankrupted his daughter. The article stated that her classmates teased her endlessly about her father's suicide and that she, too, attempted suicide more than once while in high school. She was in big trouble early on. When her father killed himself, her ability to take the life of her own offspring was greatly enhanced. In a very real way, by his act of suicide, her father "killed" her when she was a child. The horror of the act "stuck" her at the emotional age of eight and kept her there. She never grew up.

Psychological dynamics may be passed from generation to generation. Her father destroyed himself. This destroyed his daughter who then destroyed her kids. The baton was passed. Horribly simple.

24

A Shrink's Eye View

Why People Think We're Nutty

People go through life with a multitude of eyeballs. Architects see structures noting design and materials; realtors look for FSBOs (for sale by owners); clergymen see the wondrous hand of God on his creation, or they see the mark of the Devil—depending on their bent. Judges look for precedents; lawyers look for loopholes; burglars look for open windows; policemen look for suspicious characters and tree trimmers look for Dutch elm disease. There are so many facets to life we can't possibly see them all, so we specialize. In the case of shrinks our eyes are on the lookout for unconscious forces. This chapter will give you an idea how I, as a psychoanalyst, view some aspects of everyday life.

A few years ago I visited Egypt, a country that can rightfully claim to be a birthplace of Western civilization. (Don't tell the Greeks.) Much to their credit the modern Egyptians are scrupulously preserving and renovating many of the ancient monuments and structures built thousands of years ago. The first thing I noticed as we strolled among the historical buildings and ruins of ancient Egypt were the incredible number of obelisks. Obelisks, as you know, are phallic symbols. Ancient Egyptians, I decided, were pre-occupied by the penis.

There are three items to put on your "to do" list when you go to Egypt. (1) See the tombs around Luxor, (2) Take a barge ride on the Nile and (3) See the pyramids, especially the three big ones at Giza near Cairo. The laser light show at these pyramids is something to behold. Don't miss it. Visitors sit on specially constructed bleachers directly across from the pyramids as a narrative from a loudspeaker tells their fascinating story. (Be sure to attend the English version.)

From the bleachers we could faintly hear Muslim prayers being chanted, from the mosques of Cairo behind us as the laser lights in front of us meandered back and forth across the massive structures built 4,500 years ago. It was a mystical, eerie experience. Time was suspended. The sky was ablaze with stars. A warm, constant breeze came in from the desert and in my mind's eye, I could see the caravans of yore slowly and rhythmically moving across the sands. I saw Bedouin campsites and fierce Arab warriors on galloping horses with swords held high and robes flying in the wind. Soon the faces of Peter O'Toole, Elizabeth Taylor, and Charlton Heston came to mind (Lawrence of Arabia, Cleopatra, and Moses himself). Mesmerized as I was by this most special night, I couldn't help wondering what those pyramids symbolized in the unconscious minds of the ancient Egyptians. Obelisks are easy. What's a pyramid?

The narrative informed us that the pyramids were built as tombs. Each was for a specific pharaoh and its construction coincided with his rein, and this is the key: These tombs were not considered final resting places. They were designed as interim dwellings, where the pharaoh's body was interred and his spirit was readied for his next life, somewhere in the sky. The tomb, then, was a womb and through its top the pharaoh's soul would be reborn, shooting like a rocket into his new dwelling in the heavens. It was then I realized the pyramids represented upside down pubic V's—symbolizing skyward pointing vaginas. Obelisks and pyramids, penises and vaginas. It felt right to me sitting there in a birthplace of civilization.

Not long after I returned from Egypt I had a meeting in New York City with two colleagues, women psychoanalysts in their fifties. We had never met in person, although I had spoken occasionally to one on the telephone. They knew I had recently been to Egypt and politely asked about the trip. I immediately told them of all the phallic symbols in the country and shared with them my theory regarding the pyramids. My colleagues listened with interest and agreed what I said made sense, psychoanalytically speaking.

Accompanying me to this meeting was my nineteen-year-old son, Alex. At the time he thought he wanted to become a psychoanalyst.

After the meeting Alex said to me, "Dad, I can't believe you just met two women you didn't know and you started talking about penises and vaginas! And they thought it was normal. They weren't even embarrassed!" I'd never given it a second thought that ours was not a perfectly respectable conversation, and neither did they. (Alex has since decided to be a stand-up comic.)

I'm sure you've realized by now we psychoanalysts are earthy people. In the day-to-day practice of our profession we deal with gross thoughts, horrid behavior, terror, rage, nuttiness, pettiness, hatred and all things sexual. We do not deal in goodness and light. Whereas the priest may counsel with "Hail Mary, full of grace," we deal with "Hello, Mary, full of spite." The minister prays "Our father, who art in heaven." We hear "Our father was a rotten bastard." Psychotherapy is a profession immersed in emotional excrement.

One cannot go to the Middle East, by the way, without being confronted by the centuries old squabbles (hatred) among Jews, Christians and Muslims. The question of why they hate each other has been debated forever but a shrink has an easy answer. Those three religions revere the same father, Abraham. On one level, then, it's a centuries old sibling rivalry, the magnitude of hate being so great it could destroy the world. Sibling rivalries have an Oedipal element to them, however, so there's a missing entity. If dad is clearly Abraham, the question becomes, "Who is mom?" Could it be that in the collective unconscious of these three religions mom is actually God? Mothers, after all, are the real "creators" of life. Fathers have little to do with it. Muslims, Christians and Jews have been hating each other and killing each other for centuries and it isn't getting any better. Hell, it's getting worse. Only a mother could ignite, and keep aflame, such passion.

An Original Theory—I Think

Have you ever noticed that the rich people live on the north side of town and the poor people on the south side? Have you noticed that the north side is usually classier than the south side? This phenomenon, in my experience, holds true much more often than not. Whether it be big city or hamlet the rich gravitate north and the poor south. As in all human behavior there has to be an unconscious reason for this, and years ago I came up with a theory.

Our bodies have an impact on our concept of who we are. There is a saying, "The ego is a body ego." Ugly people are not as confident as good-looking ones, usually. Tall men are more contented than short men. Obese women are more self-conscious than those of average weight, etc. Before you start your next fire with this book, let me hasten to say that I've just used the loosest of generalizations and I am aware there are many exceptions.

Leaping along, if our body's configuration affects our self-image, it will also affect our actions. In all bodies we have a north and a south. In the north are a human being's riches, the one and only thing that makes us superior to other mammals—our minds. In the south are our genitals which are no more effective than those of the turtles. So if you're "movin' on up" … you're moving north.

Even in our little southern town my theory holds true. For instance, North Main Street is all spiffed up. South Main Street looks like shit. The same syndrome is readily demonstrated in my hometown, Chicago. The Northsiders eat quiche, sip chardonnay and politely cheer for the Cubs. They are genteel people. On the Southside we find White Sox fans who gorge on hot dogs, chug-a-lug beer and holler obscenities at opposing players. They are barbarians. I expounded on my theory at a dinner party one night and a man from Boston got so upset with me he grabbed his wife and left. I never found out which side of town he lived on.

Of course, my theory has more holes than a golf course and it cannot be proven that there is an unconscious motivation to move north when affluence is acquired. And I really don't care if my theory is correct or not. It's fun to observe this north-south tendency and it's the kind of stuff I think about.

You've Been Named

I do not have a hobby. I play racquetball, golf, and walk three miles a day with my dogs, but that's exercise, not a hobby. The closest thing I have to a real hobby is collecting names. I have a file full of them because I believe people's names can unconsciously influence them, particularly with their career choice. This is no doubt a throwback to earlier times when the Masons were masons, Carpenters were carpenters, Barbers were barbers, Bakers were bakers, Millers were millers, Farmers were farmers, and there was a Smithy on every corner.

In my file, for instance, is Dr. Cynthia Earle, who runs an ad on our local T.V. Hearing problem? She can fix you right up. I wrote a letter once to Dr. Buzz Aldren, the second astronaut to walk on the moon. I asked if he thought, perhaps unconsciously, his mother's maiden name influenced his career choice. Her name is Marion Moon. He did not write back. Maybe he didn't get the letter.

There's a slew of names in my file of those who work with nature. Fred Bear the famous hunter and Joe Wolfe the gifted dog handler are there, as are Art Wolfe the nature photographer and Howard Fox the forester. In a single article in *National Geographic* I read about James Fish of the Naval Undersea Research and Development Center in San Diego and Marie Fish, a marine scientist from the University of Rhode Island. Mr. Joel Parrott is the executive director of the Oakland Zoo, by the way.

In Georgetown, South Carolina, the director of the St. Francis Humane Society is Pert Shelter. (Close enough.) In Polk County, North Carolina, a volunteer at its humane society is Ms. Kitty Holder. Mr. Ni Juin Fang broke the world's record for living with poisonous snakes in a cage. Lastly, in this category, up in Manitoba, Canada, a record moose was taken by one Dan Hill. His Indian guide was Victor Moose.

Ms. Linda Sweeting is a chemist. Her specialty is studying sweets. Bill McNutt is the president of a fruitcake company. Michael Fairclothe designs clothes. Ronnie Lamb sells cashmere and Eric Flaxenburg sells wool. Ed Van Artsdale sells vans. Tiger Woods is a golfer. Oral Roberts is a preacher.

If you pay attention to names linked with occupations you'll see them frequently but names may have other influences. A chef, Satir Konstas, resides on Fork Circle in Elgin, Illinois. Tom Forka is the co-founder of the Waffle House restaurant chain. I read with amusement that the famous feminist Gloria Steinam has a best friend named Wilma

Mankiller. (This probably has no meaning.) Even an entire community might be affected by its name. Hightstown, New Jersey, for instance, bought a new fire truck that could reach blazes up to 135 feet. The tallest building in town is forty feet.

And names could be prophetic in other ways. A magazine special on obesity had an interview with a man who was about to embark on a crash diet because he said he'd gotten too fat to play with his grandchildren. His last name was Pappaphat. Lastly, (this could go on forever), a name may determine whom we marry. When Ezra Pound was a budding writer, he took Dorothy Shakespeare to be his wife.

I also have fun observing how people show their unconscious minds. I note the narcissist by his frequent use of the pronoun "I." I see the cheapskate get preoccupied when the check arrives and watch the insecure guy grab it. I pay attention to those who won't look me, or a camera, in the eye. They've got a secret. I've observed that incessant talkers don't want to hear anything new. They've already heard something terrible. Those, of course, are only clues to personality glitches and taken alone have little value. But sometimes a person's unconscious is openly displayed as in the uniform he wears. I don't mean the mandatory uniform of his profession—policeman, airline pilot, circus clown, etc.—I mean the uniform he chooses to wear. One time my son, Walter, and I went on a fishing trip, just the two of us. He had learned that he was going to be a father for the first time and wanted to spend some time with me. When the big day arrived I picked up Walter and we headed to "The Preserve." We got there in time for supper.

The main dining hall had a rustic wood motif. Taxidermied fish and animals native to the area adorned the walls. A large fireplace, a regulation size pool table, comfortable, over-stuffed chairs and a great view of the lake welcomed visitors. In the center of the room circular dining tables were set for dinner—cloth napkins folded into peaks and long stemmed wine glasses. This was nice, certainly not roughing it, and all very civilized except for one thing. The other guests, now seated at the tables, were dressed in camouflage outfits. Every one of them. Not only could guests fish at The Preserve but also hunt, and we were in the middle of deer, duck and wild boar season.

The Preserve is not cheap (upwards of $1,000 per day if you are hunting with a guide), so it was safe to assume the guests were men of means, sitting at their tables wearing matching hats, shirts, pants and even boots. They looked ready to embark for Desert Storm. "Look at the kids," I said to Walter, "they're playing Army."

Walter, a nice young man, tried to defend the men's uniforms by saying they wore camouflage so the deer wouldn't see them. I told him deer were mostly colorblind, the hunters could be wearing bright pink polo shirts and it wouldn't matter. The dressed-up hunters were engaging in what shrinks call "regression in the service of the ego." They were regressing, going back in time when their unconscious minds were formed, letting an unresolved part of it show itself. Titans of industry on the outside, little kid Rambos inside and no harm done. In fact, their outings and outfits were therapy. Being suited up in camouflage, they were getting off their frustrated urges to be he-man killers—a stage every little boy goes through. So it's good to vent the latent aggression on ducks, bucks and boar rather than on wives, kids and employees.

Don't Bring Your Family to Work

Speaking of employees, since I backed off from full-time practice and entered business I have had dozens of them. Invariably they squabbled among themselves and frequently sought me out to privately complain about one another. I simply listened. The workplace is an unconscious extension of the family environment. The employees are siblings and I'm dad. My analytic background was valuable in helping me see this relationship and, therefore, not overreact to intra-office bickering.

Sometimes employees told me other employees were saying negative things about me, in effect ratting out their "brothers and sisters." I would listen then say something like, "I'm sorry they feel that way." To myself I would say, "Who cares what they say about me as long as they're doing their jobs." Being aware of the transference and not taking their words personally helped me stay focused on the mission at hand—making money. That's what a business is supposed to do.

Many businesses pride themselves on being "like family." I've always felt that was a bad idea. The family is a competitive organization with the kids vying for their parents' attention and often the parents vying with each other for their children's love and respect. This does not represent a good business model. Besides, half the families in America break up. I see no benefit and many pitfalls to encouraging employees to think of their company as family. Often their family experience was not a happy one and they'll unconsciously re-create that dynamic in the workplace.

Business is about money; money comes from sales, and sales come from salespeople. Most salespeople are awful. They talk too much! They have the misguided idea that good salesmen are good talkers when just the opposite is true. It is the customers who should be talking. Salespeople should ask their customers and prospective customers about themselves, their spouses, their kids, their pets, their hobbies. They should listen carefully to what is being said and take notes afterwards. Before long these customers will think the salespeople are not only the nicest people they know but also the best conversationalists. The best salespeople do the least amount of talking. They ask questions and then they shut up. Just like shrinks.

25

The Final Session

RES

It's almost time for resolution and termination, but first some housekeeping. You should know I do not believe Adam and Eve are historical. I was taught Darwin's theory of biological evolution by the Jesuits and that's how I perceive life on our planet. I also believe in the theory of spiritual evolution convincingly put forth by the paleontologist Pierre Teihard De Chardin (It's a tossup to see which is moving at the slower pace.)

But Adam and Eve metaphorically suited my purposes so I used them throughout the book. Everybody in Western civilization knows their story. Psychoanatically speaking they were the first "undoers." They had it made in the Garden of Eden. There was only one thing God forbade them to do and, of course, they did it. Their first two children engaged in the first sibling rivalry. It ended in murder. The Adam and Eve Family was dysfunctional, desperately in need of therapy.

Nor do I believe in the devil, although I used him also. The devil is a religious concept to describe that part of *every unconscious mind* which is self serving, greedy, spiteful, hateful and malicious—words we use to describe evil. The devil's name is not Beelzebub or Lucifer. It is Id.

I do believe in God but wouldn't attempt to describe this being except to say that love, beauty and truth seem to emanate from that existence. I believe we humans are drawn toward a relationship with God but I've only the tiniest grasp of what that means. (And the id diligently discourages that quest.) And I believe in miracles.

My colleague, Dr. Margery Quackenbush of New York, wrote her Ph.D. thesis on the exciting new field of neuroscience. In her thesis she states (I paraphrase) that it has been found that psychotherapy alone, without accompanying medications, can positively alter brain functions. "Psychotherapy can re-wire the brain," she writes. In other words a spiritual interaction where only words and feelings are exchanged between two people can alter the workings of a physical organ. That's a miracle.

At the Lucy Daniels Center, a psychoanalytic institute in North Carolina, I heard the well known psychiatrist, psychoanalyst and author Glen Gabbard, M.D., state the same thing, adding that newly devised monitoring equipment scientifically proves it. That is wonderful news for us talk therapists and our patients, although we're always believed this was so.

The temptation, then, would be to declare war on drugs and throw them out. But, for at least three reasons, that would be stupid: (1) The depths of psychotherapeutic treatments vary dramatically. (2) The expertise of psychotherapists vary even more dramatically. (3) Medications work. They, too, can positively alter brain functioning and they can do it a lot faster than talk therapy.

When I began analytic training we were taught that medications for almost all mental problems were not only unnecessary but were copouts. Traditional analysts thought that mental illness could be talked away given enough time, the proper setting, and a solid connect between analyst and analysand. Only the most seriously ill would be allowed drugs. For many years I believed this (I only resorted to them once) but not anymore. Medications are not always a cop-out.

Medications available today can lift depression, rein in mania, stabilize moods, and correct crazy thoughts often in just a few days. To not use them in certain instances would be cruel to the patients and irresponsible on the part of the therapist.

But it is important to keep in mind that medications will not cure mental illness anymore than insulin cures diabetes. They merely keep the condition in check and medications should not be used alone. A pill's properties don't include insights and they cannot make interpretations—the stuff of permanent healing and growth. Nor do medications change personalities: The nice remain nice; the jerks remain jerks.

The Mind and I

A medication's most important function is as a catalyst for connecting with another soul, allowing for a therapeutic relationship. That will be the deepest and most personal relationship someone will ever have, which is the main healing force, the ultimate butt saver.

As to the cause of mental illness, I am a believer that most are environmentally based. After reading this book you certainly know that. But there are other factors to consider. Let's return to words from Dr. Quackenbush: "We are just beginning to explore the structural organization of the brain ... instead of distinguishing between mental disorders along biologic and non-biologic lines, it might be more appropriate to ask ... to what degree is the biologic process determined by genetic and developmental factors, to what degree is it due to infections or toxic agents, and to what degree is it socially determined?"

Fair enough. We still have a lot to learn. But in the meantime let's hear about the patient's mom and dad. Even if they've had nothing to do with his emotional problems (impossible) we'll learn more about the total person.

A little more housekeeping. I have not been overly kind to my fellow mental health professionals. Let me set that record straight. Most I know are good, solid, caring people who are trustworthy and know what they're doing. But the field does attract some goofy people. Recently I was on a cruise boat for a week with perhaps fifty passengers. On the first night one of them confided to me: "I'm a psychotherapist but don't tell anybody. I don't want people bothering me while I'm on vacation." (I didn't tell her I was an analyst.) She got drunk every night and by the end of the week had "confided" this tidbit to the other forty-nine people on board. They were laughing about it behind her back. She was goofy.

On the other hand, being goofy is not always bad. I have a professional artist friend whom most people would consider strange. (Of course he's strange—he's an artist.) We hadn't been in contact for many years but recently reconnected. I asked him if he'd been helped by psychoanalysis some twenty years before. I knew his analyst who was also strange. "Yeah, he helped me a lot. It takes a crazy fucker to help another crazy fucker," he said. There's truth there.

The mental health community is splintered into numerous schools of thought each believing they've got "the answer," mirroring my experience with my Goddard College classmates of years ago. These schools are a parochial bunch and quarrels are frequent. This doesn't bother me; there's nothing wrong with scholarly fights, and good ideas may result. I'm glad Carl Jung broke with Freud, for instance, adding another dimension to psychoanalysis. What does bother me is that many psychological schools concentrate solely on conscious thought and behavior, which are *symptoms* of deeper problems. They treat them and stop. They seemed to have lost the knack, or knowledge, to get into the unconscious mind of their patients where *causes* dwell. That's a dangerous trend away from psychic reality and seems to be an embracement of society's reality today, you know, shallow. Treating symptoms merely creates different symptoms, shifting them around. The causes remain, firing away, not really caring how they are manifested. If people go through life in touch with their conscious minds only, they have missed much of the journey.

Lastly, a word to my patients. You allowed me to participate in your most private, intimate thoughts and feelings. You humbled me by your trust. As the years go by and I reflect on our times together that humility deepens and, as you may recall, humility was not one of my virtues.

I know that some of you would not have minded seeing yourselves in the book by name and having your therapy sessions described in detail. (Some of you would have loved it.) I couldn't do that, of course. However, you are all in the book in essence. You were my ultimate teachers, daily proving the commonality of the unconscious minds of Everyone. You enriched my life, and I am forever grateful.

Okay, that's it. I've said what I wanted to say in this book. Please remember that even though you've read it from cover to cover your emotional system has not been improved. If you think it needs improving see a shrink. One who cares. One who listens.

Bibliography

(Suggested Reading)

Brenner, Charles. *An Elementary Textbook of Psychoanalysis*. New York: Anchor, 1974.

Freud, Sigmund. *The Interpretation of Dreams*. Translated by A. A. Brill. New York: Macmillan, 1913.

Jung, C. G. *Man and His Symbols*. New York: Dell, 1964.

Lidz, Theodore. *The Person*. New York: Basic, 1976.

Lindner, Robert. *The Fifty Minute Hour*. New York: Other Press, 1999.

Malcolm, Janet. *Psychoanalysis: The Impossible Profession*. New York: Knopf, 1981.

Roazen, Paul. *Freud and His Followers*. New York: Knopf, 1975.

Shem, Samuel. *Mount Misery*. New York: Bantam, 2003.

Teilhard de Chardin, Pierre. *The Divine Milieu*. Toronto: Sussex Academic Press, 2004.

Yalom, Irvin. *When Nietzsche Wept*. New York: Basic, 1992.

Index

Index